## Contents

# INTRODUCTION

## John Hipkin

THIS BOOK IS a compilation of some of the best articles on pre-schooling to have appeared in WHERE during the last ten years. In planning the book and starting work on it, we saw it in the main as being a practical guide to parents who wanted to understand better the educational needs of their young children and who wanted to know how best to meet those needs. In essence this is what the book has become. However, as the book took shape we also saw that, without consciously intending it, it was by way of being a tribute to the pre-school movement in Britain which developed with such vigour in the early 1960s at about the time that ACE itself was set up.

**Official aid or self-help?**

That movement can justifiably take credit for some quite extraordinary achievements, the foremost of which has been the involvement of literally thousands of parents in pre-school cooperatives. Thus rather than wait for desultory and equivocal governments to give a lead and produce the resources which the nation's parents and their young children have needed and still need, parents themselves, often unaided and unacknowledged, have taken the initiative by setting up hundreds of playgroups, nurseries and day-care centres which they have administered, staffed and largely financed themselves.

Comparisons, we know, are odious and we would not want to overlook the contribution to pre-schooling which both central and local government have made, particularly with respect to needy and handicapped children. But placed beside the record of the parentally fostered pre-school movement, the investment by government in the care and education of the under-fives has been pitifully inadequate.

In the early 1970s there was evidence of a real change of heart by government. The 1972 White Paper *A framework for expansion* proposed an appreciable expansion of nursery schooling in the seventies and beyond, and in the following year discretionary grants to the tune of £34 million were offered to local education authorities to enable them to provide 70,000 extra nursery places. This commitment to improved pre-school education was endorsed by each of the major political parties at the time of the subsequent general elections, and hopes were therefore high that by the end of the decade a high proportion of British families would receive the benefit of government-provided nursery schooling. In the event, however, these hopes have been largely disappointed. Cuts in public expenditure earlier this year now make it certain that far from there being any expansion in nursery provision it will be difficult even to maintain the meagre supply of existing places. It is also clear that much of the money made available to LEAs for the expansion of nursery schooling will go unspent, since LEAs claim they cannot afford to match the grants offered by the Department of Education and Science (DES).

As so often before, then, the nation's principal hope for development and expansion in the pre-school field now lies with parents, and as this book demonstrates, we may expect that challenge, whatever the shortages and difficulties may be, to be taken up with vigour and imagination by the parents of Britain. It is to be hoped that their example will sooner rather than later galvanise policy-makers into playing their full part.

**ACE's contribution to the pre-school movement**

ACE is proud to have played a part in the growth of the pre-school movement. In one of the first editions of WHERE (**8**, 1962) Belle Tutaev, who is widely renowned as the moving spirit of the pre-school movement, announced the setting up of the Pre-school Playgroups Association (PPA). Thousands of parents followed in her footsteps and by 1973 there were 250,000 children attending playgroups in membership of the PPA. Today the figures stand at almost 400,000. The collection of articles contained in this book, together with the many others on pre-school playgroups which have appeared in WHERE, but which it has not been possible to include, are testimony to the support which ACE has given and still gives to the PPA.

In 1964 the National Extension College (set up by ACE a year earlier) launched the first ever correspondence course for parents on playgroups. The course was designed by Elizabeth Matterson, the then chairman of the PPA, and for several years it was linked to a series of BBC radio programmes. The NEC, which is now an independent body, reports that the pre-school course still has a sizeable following and will remain part of its programme. (Interested parents should write to the National Extension College, 131 Hills Road, Cambridge CB2 1PD.)

ACE's own nursery school was set up in Cambridge in the Spring of 1966. Janet Weinroth, who contributes the article on children's painting on page 14, was its first director. In many ways the ACE nursery school was a breakthrough for it showed that between the state nursery school proper, with its own professional staff and official backing, and the wholly parent-run playgroup there was a need for a nursery school which incorporated the best features of both; a full-time qualified staff providing a rich educational environment and programme of learning together with the active involvement of parents. For ten years the ACE nursery school has gathered strength and under the direction of Monique Turpin, her staff and parents, it continues to provide uniquely valuable service.

In 1968 ACE's interest in the pre-school movement took a different and exciting turn. The Multi-Racial Playgroups Association was formed in association with the Indian Workers' Committee and the Race Relations Committee of the Society of Friends. The purpose of the Association was to set up playgroups for children of different races living in what the Plowden Report called 'educational priority areas' (EPAs). The David Gretton Nursery in Birmingham was the first of the Associ-

# The best of where on pre-schooling

Advisory Centre for Education

Advisory Centre for Education
Dr White House
32 Trumpington Street
Cambridge CB2 1QY

The best of WHERE on pre-schooling

ISBN 0 900029 46 3



Printed in England
by Heffers Printers Ltd, Cambridge

Cover photograph by Lorna Minton

ation's playgroups and this was followed two years later by a group based on the Mount Pleasant Community Centre, also in Birmingham. Other groups were set up under the aegis of the MRPA and the newly formed Priority Area Playgroups. When Dr Eric Midwinter's EPA Project joined forces with ACE in 1972 further support was given to a number of pre-school projects in Liverpool.

ACE greeted the 1972 White Paper's promise of a greatly expanded nursery education programme with some scepticism. Writing in the December 1973 issue of WHERE, Beryl McAlhone asked for 'a scrupulous reappraisal of the kind of provision that is needed'. With her characteristic command of facts and figures she was able to show that government money for nursery schooling might not reach in sufficient quantities those parts of the country which needed it most. Looking back, Beryl's doubts seem to have been more than justified.

**The present position**

What is the present state of pre-schooling in this country? I began this introduction by paying tribute to the mainly voluntary efforts of those parents who have brought about one of the most remarkable of developments in modern education: the birth and growth of the PPA. I have acknowledged too, the part, albeit sadly inadequate, played by government in the development of pre-schooling. But having taken account of the contributions of both parents acting in concert and of government, pre-school care and education in Britain is still shamefully inadequate.

What are the facts? Of the two and a half million children aged between two and four in England and Wales only 14 per cent receive any kind of full-time pre-school education, and of these only 4·7 per cent are in nursery schools. The majority attend nursery classes within primary schools. A further 78,000 under-fives receive part-time nursery education in maintained nursery schools and classes. This leaves two million children not catered for by the state system. Numbers of places, mainly part-time, provided by the voluntary bodies, the PPA, Save the Children, the Women's Royal Voluntary Service and others, are difficult to estimate but their total contribution, magnificent as it is, is still likely to be under one third of a million places. This means that more than 75 per cent of the nation's under-fives are still without any kind of pre-schooling.

Ron Chapman

At this point it needs to be said that the present patterns and policies in pre-school care and education may not be the best ones, and it would be unwise, therefore, simply to urge for expansion on all fronts equally. Clearly careful account must be taken of how different possible strategies for pre-schooling will affect the lives of individual parents, families and communities. However, even when allowance has been made for the need continually to question the deployment of resources there can be no doubt that the total level of pre-school provision at the present time is grossly inadequate.

The consequences of this neglect bear hardest, of course, upon the families affected. And here it should be said that parents want proper care and education for their children, including their youngest children, not in order to shuffle off their responsibilities as parents, but in order to cope more effectively with increasing demands and pressures upon them.

What are these demands and pressures? First, an increasing number of mothers of young children go out to work. In part this trend reflects hard economic realities – families often need the income of two breadwinners if they are to maintain, let alone improve, their living standards. This is particularly true during a period of economic recession when real incomes may actually be falling, but even in better times the expense of caring for a growing family puts very heavy strains upon the family budget. Second, and perhaps of even greater long-term significance, women are increasingly demanding the same social and economic rights as men. Among the most important of such rights is that of taking up a career (as opposed to a job) and of developing an identity which is not exclusively tied to housekeeping and child-rearing. Failure to acknowledge the changing attitudes to sex-roles in our society and failure to make provision for these changes will undoubtedly contribute to tensions and problems of a kind that affect all members of the family, but most of all, perhaps, the youngest children. Third, urban life, particularly in excessively crowded areas or in places denuded of social relationships (in high-rise flats, for example) means that mothers need opportunities for significant contact with other people. Being involved in the education of their children, especially in the way that parents in playgroups are, provides one kind of shared activity, the value of which is beyond dispute.

Finally, parents are increasingly conscious of how important the early years of childhood are and there is a growing recognition that parental attitudes and values are an integral part of the child's healthy development. But most parents cannot discharge all their responsibilities without qualified guidance, support and assistance. This, we insist, does not imply a breakdown of family life, or an abdication of responsibility by parents; it reflects, rather, the growing complexity of the task of bringing up children today.

We have spoken so far of the needs of parents. But the children of this country are not solely the responsibility of their parents. A modern society must accept that the care and education of young children is a community as well as a family responsibility and that to fail this trust will have serious implications for the country as a whole. Mothers need to work, but equally, their work is needed by the nation, and the nation must make it possible for women to work without continually worrying whether their children are being adequately cared for and educated.

There is also abundant evidence that the quality of parental interest in a child's education is the foremost factor influencing a child's progress at school. Clearly the nation needs a well-educated population, living as it does mainly on the skills of its people, so that the involvement of ordinary parents in their children's education must represent a considerable bonus for the country as a whole. Research and common sense combine to tell us that the foundations of personality and social attitudes are laid in the home. But coming into the home and closely interwined with the family are a host of outside factors: the quality of one's working life; pay and prospects; contacts with friends, neighbours and official bodies; opportunities for rest and recreation; and the education of one's children. If any of these are absent or inadequate the neglect is registered in the child's developing personality. No-one can estimate accurately how great the cost to society is of an under-investment in our children's welfare and education. But the cost is unacceptably high.

**A policy for pre-schooling**

ACE has called before and calls again for a coherent policy for pre-school education. The aim of this policy must be the provision of pre-school education for all the children who need it or whose parents wish for it. Naturally such a policy cannot be implemented overnight, especially during a time of economic austerity. But a firm commitment to the objective of pre-school education for all who seek it is possible and should be given in the most unequivocal terms. Plans should also be laid for moving as rapidly as possible toward this objective. We need a thorough-going reappraisal of the whole field of pre-school care and education to determine what might be the most effective strategies in the years ahead. Teacher-training courses also need to be steadily adapted in readiness for the enlarged investment in pre-school education.

Deciding upon priorities must also be urgently undertaken. ACE believes that when the pre-school programme is once again accelerated resources should go first to those areas – particularly inner city areas – where need is greatest. Area by area surveys to determine the extent and character of this need should be immediately embarked upon. Rather than full-time nursery education for a small minority of children it may make good sense to give more children part-time pre-schooling. There should also be a sorting out of responsibilities for pre-schooling as between the DES, the DHSS and the Home Office. None of these measures can be ruled out on the grounds of cost. Indeed vigorously and thoroughly pursued they could eventually ensure a much more cost-effective investment of resources.

Britain, we are well aware, is passing through a troubled phase in its history and many of the good things in life which are the product of growing wealth may have to be sacrificed in the immediate future. But how a society responds to crisis and misfortune, and what it holds true to during such times is the real test of its claim to be civilised. In our view the commitment to public education must be among a society's most cherished principles and since the child's early years are so important to his subsequent development improved pre-school care and provision ought to be the very first of the nation's educational priorities in the years ahead.

*John Hipkin was director of ACE from May 1974 to August 1976.*

Rob Bray

# 1 How children learn

# LEARNING TO SPEAK

## Hunter Diack

IT IS A common assumption that a child's education really begins when he makes his first steps in reading. That is a fallacy. His first steps in reading may indeed fairly well coincide with the beginning of his formal education, but his basic education began long before that. Indeed it could be argued that in the years between 12 months and five years he makes a greater educational advance than he will make in any subsequent period of similar duration.

It is during that period that he breaks through the sound barrier, learns to speak effectively. At the beginning of that period his behaviour bears a considerable resemblance to that of a highly intelligent chimpanzee; by the end of that period that comparison becomes something like sacrilege.

In learning to speak the child is learning to think, to perceive, to classify his perceptual experiences, to enter into relationships with other human beings and to engage in all the other activities which set human beings so decisively apart from all the other inhabitants of this planet. It is through speech that the child acquires his store of meanings. Unless a word has been encountered in speech it will mean nothing or very little to him, even long after he has learned to read. Even with adults it is on the whole true to say that anyone who cannot put into his own spoken words anything that he has read has not understood it but has allowed the print to drift through his mind.

**'Inner speech'**

Speech is the fundamental thing about language. That is where the meanings lie. In order to understand the printed word the child has to translate print into speech. At first he has to read aloud. Later he will read silently, but he will be thinking in words, the words of what is called 'inner speech.'

These facts give a fairly solid foundation for the statement that a child who has rich language experience during his pre-school years has acquired a solid basis for his further development. They do not, however, give any basis for trying to get your child to speak earlier than the child next door or for worrying because your infant has not yet said his first word even though he is three months older than you were when, according to your mother, you were already a little chatterbox.

You can pretty well discount any statement you hear about when you, or anyone else, first spoke an intelligible word. There are several reasons for the wisdom of this scepticism. The two most important are that it is very easy for parents to read meanings into sounds a baby makes and to call these sounds words, though nobody else would, and that it is very common for a child to make sounds that coincide with the sounds of accepted words – for example, it is widely agreed among experts in this field that the words 'mama' and 'dada' were taken over by adults from the child's natural repertoire of sounds. Certainly an infant will make sounds that are meaningful to his mother, and his mother may legitimately claim that he is speaking. Until he is making sounds that are meaningful to people other than herself, however, she can hardly claim that he is yet speaking English.

For a considerable part of his first year of life the infant spends a fair amount of his time playing at making sounds. This play is important in his progress towards speech. His first sounds are, of course, sounds of protest; silence in the first week or two means sleep or contentment. Soon, however, he falls into the habit of cooing, crooning and gurgling in his state of contentment. He appears to get pleasure out of the sound of his own voice; he experiments in the making of sounds. It has been said that by the time a baby is nine months old he will normally have produced at one time or another all the vowel sounds and most of the consonantal sounds in the English language and some that are not in the English language at all. It is a remarkable thing, however, that even at so early an age the sounds he makes will have a tendency to resemble the sounds characteristic of the language he hears around him. A tape recording of the sounds made by a Japanese baby three weeks old, for example, will be indistinguishable from one made of the sounds produced by an English baby, but the same will not be true when the babies are two or three months older. Even before the first distinguishable word has been spoken, the child's repertoire of sounds is being influenced by the sounds made by the human beings in his immediate environment. This implies at least a rudimentary imitation of the sounds he hears in the world around him.

We usually notice imitation only when it is reasonably successful. When we are considering imitation in the context of child development, however, we have to take a wider view of it than that. Close students of the development of speech in children have pointed out that there is a rudimentary imitation when a child responds to a sound with any other sound at all. If he responded to a voice merely by waggling his toes and smiling, that would not be called imitation even in its most rudimentary form, but a response of sound to sound shows that the imitative process has definitely begun.

Another point of some importance for the understanding of these first stages of speech-development is that when the child is at his babbling play he is learning how to imitate others by imitating himself. At least that is how it seems. Listen to the babbling of a child in a cot and you will hear a great many repetitions of particular sounds and of combinations of sounds. The frequency of repetitive combinations like 'mama,' 'dada,' 'gaga' and 'baba' may indicate the infant's inborn love of rhythm, as has frequently been claimed, but that does not remove this sort of voice behaviour from the context of imitation. What is rhythm but a kind of imitation, imitation of the sound or movement that has gone before?

**Don't confuse mimicry with intelligence**

The best mimics are the most likely to show

From WHERE 35 (January 1968)

the earliest signs of progress towards speech. There is not, however, a close connection between ability as a mimic and intelligence. Therefore the parent of a child who learns to speak his first words at an unusually early age has no right to expect equally rapid progress on the intellectual front generally. Nor, on the other hand, should the parents of a child who is slow to break through the sound barrier jump easily or early to the conclusion that he is going to be a slow learner in other directions. I am not arguing that he speaks best who learns to speak last, but I would certainly stand by the statement that the early speaker does not necessarily have the last word.

The role of the parents at this early stage is of paramount importance – particularly the role of the mother. The infant should not only be hearing talk but should also see himself being talked to. Baby-talk, *ie* 'mummy-talk' by the mother to her baby, is often the subject of satirical skits – unworthily. Fortunately no mother is likely to be put off by that. It is, of course, a great mistake for a mother to carry on the habit of baby-talk after an infant has learned to speak a fair number of English words in the normal manner, but at the very earliest stages of speech, baby-talk has several important functions:

☐ In using the repetitive words of baby-talk, the mother is fitting her language to the natural rhythms of the infant's babbling period and is thus giving the child easy practice in imitation.

☐ She is forming a series of sound-bonds between the child and herself, thus giving the sounds an emotional meaning.

☐ She is linking specific sounds to the child's experience of the world apart from her and outside himself in the easiest possible way. Take 'bow-wow,' for example: here we have a sound with a repetitive pattern which in itself can be pronounced in such a way as to link it naturally with the sound a dog makes. Excellent teaching technique.

To continue this kind of language too long, however, is not good. The child who takes baby-talk to school – and there are

some of these unfortunates in nearly every large infant class – may be held up to ridicule by his more mature-speaking classmates. The common language is his passport to entry to the new society of the school. Do not blot it by teaching him to cling to the semi-private language of babyhood. I'm referring here not only to the 'bow-wow' 'tootsie-wootsie' 'moo-cow' sort of baby talk, but also the special names that children may give to things – 'nano' for piano say. When a child makes these early and often charming attempts at words they are frequently adopted by the family as well. But to preserve a child's early attempts at speech up to the time when he is due to go to school is to treat him very much as a toy you don't want to lose.

Parents who encourage their children to talk sometimes quite unwittingly make things difficult for them. This difficulty is often caused by the nature of the language itself. Something in the language being used may set his mind off on the wrong track. An example: a mother once, rather thoughtlessly, said to a young child, 'watch the milk!' The milk was in a pan on the stove. The milk boiled over – and the child, obediently, watched it. There was no need for that mother to be annoyed with the child for not calling out that the milk was boiling over. The child's experience of language was such as to make it impossible for her to think: 'when my mother asks me to watch the milk, she does not mean me to watch the milk, but to run and tell her when it boils over.'

It is often said that children have a logic of their own. In every instance I have ever come across where it seemed as though the child's logic was different, I have found that it was not the logic that was different but the *experience of things and of language* that was limited. The child who looks for a 'snow-bow' in the sky is not being silly, nor particularly imaginative; he is being logical. The child has been told about, and seen, a rainbow, why should there not be a 'snow-bow'? It would be better for the adult to explain why not – if he can! – than to think of the comment as one of the quaint illogicality of the infant mind.

A golden rule for the parent or the adult who has to deal with children is to assume that where a child has not understood, the fault is not in the child but in the adult who has assumed too much experience. For it is in experience of things and of words connected with things that understanding lies.

Usually if a parent speaks clearly, the child will acquire a habit of clear speech too. Clear speech, however, does not mean loud speech. How many adults have frightened children by half-shouting at them in the mistaken idea that mere volume makes sound clearer?

Where a child does pronounce certain words badly, the attentive parent will naturally try to get him to correct the mistake. This should be done gently, however. Keep nagging at him and you are more likely to do harm than good, making him self-conscious and unwilling to speak. Nursery rhymes clearly spoken and chanted by the child are a great aid to clear speech.

Two final points: the child who gets everything he wants without ever having to ask for it will be slow to learn how useful language is as a means of getting what you want.

The child who gets few responses to the sounds he makes will also be slow to learn that words bring results. The happy medium between anticipating his needs and ignoring his requests is best.

Peter Eastland

# LEARNING TO READ

## Hunter Diack

'IN SPITE OF what you say I have no intention of stopping teaching my baby how to read.' That sentence comes from a letter I had from a mother who was teaching her child of about two and a half how to read. She added: 'Both she and I enjoy it too much.' She was writing to me after having read a pamphlet I wrote for *Family Doctor* in which I had urged parents to be cautious about a craze that seemed to be developing at the time as the result of the publication of a book about teaching babies to read. No great harm can be done by playing word and letter games even with children so very young, provided they simply are games and are not taken too seriously by the parent. The fact that these games are called 'teaching my baby to read' seems to me to bring an ominous note into the situation.

It is highly desirable that parents should have some knowledge of what is going on when a child is learning to read and so I am going to set down in short numbered sections what seems to me the minimum information about the process that a parent should possess.

**What any parent should know**

**1** – It is true that many children (indeed most children) will be found recognising whole words in print, if they are told what the words are, before they know anything about letters. This is simple commonsense. My reason for pointing it out is to emphasise that this uninformed recognising of words should not be regarded as reading. The danger of regarding it as reading is that if you do so you begin to expect the child to make much quicker progress than is within his powers and begin to show impatience when the apparently early promise is slow in being fulfilled.

**2** – This early recognition of whole words is not to be taken to imply that the child is seeing the words with the clarity and definition of which you, the adult, are capable. The usual thing is that he has seized on part of a word and associated that part with the sound of the whole word, and, of course, if it is in his meaningful vocabulary, with the meaning as well. If a little boy called James has learned to recognise his name in print and he sees the word 'Jumbo' in a story book, he is quite likely to point to Jumbo and say: 'That is James'. It is fairly obvious that there is a good chance in that case that he has fixed on the capital J as being the main indication of 'James'.

**3** – The real stage of learning to read occurs when the child is learning to translate the letters in a word into the correct sounds, in the correct order, and then associating the sound of the word with the meaning. Now this is a slow process and the very slowness of it, contrasted with the apparent speed with which the child learnt whole words, may lead to a fair amount of upset in both parent and child. It is not unusual for a child who has learned to recognise as many as 50 words by the age of, say, three and a half, to be unable to understand the significance of letters for another two to three years. Small wonder that many parents who are aglow with the early success of their young readers get depressed about the slowness of the progress later on.

**4** – Some parents teach their children to read by the oldest of all methods – spelling out simple words to children using the alphabetic names of the letters. That drilling method is hardly ever used nowadays in schools; one reason is that there is no apparent connection between, say, the sounds see-ey-tee and the sound of the whole word 'cat'. On the other hand there is not a very clear connection between the sounds ker-a-ter and the sound of the whole word 'cat'. The old alphabetic or spelling method has never been proved a failure, but on the other hand some modern methods are better.

**5** – A phonic method is one in which the child is taught the sounds the letters stand for. There are obvious difficulties here. One of them has already been indicated in the statement that 'ker-a-ter' does not sound like 'cat' – or at least not very like it. I have heard children say, 'ber-er-ker-yer ker-ler-er – bicycle' which just shows you how incredibly accommodating children can be. But here we have a real difficulty, the fact that English is so irregularly spelt.

**6** – The main difficulty of the real learning to read stage is getting the child to blend the separate letter-sounds into words. That is why with really backward children I have tried using words in which the sounds represented by the letters easily blend together: for example, the word 'man' which is spoken to the child not as mer-a-ner, as I have sometimes heard, but as m–m–m–a–n-n-n, the separate letters being indicated by the finger, then written separately as m a n, brought closer together and said more quickly m a n, and finally printed and spoken normally. Starting in that way with a boy of 11 who had been six years at school and remained unable to read a single word, I went through the following succession in the slow way suggested above: man, an, and, sun, sand. The whole thing took 20 minutes and the last word he read by himself, the very first word he had ever read. Once a child – and I am not now speaking of very backward children – has got insight into the function of letters, he will usually make rapid progress given suitable books to read. But it cannot be too strongly emphasised that this stage of getting to understand what the letters stand for is the crucial stage in learning to read.

**When to start**

Such then are some of the essential facts about what one may call the mechanical side of reading. What about the timing of the process? When should a child begin to learn to read? That's the commonest question I am asked about this subject, and my commonest answer is: 'It depends'. Some educational writers, appalled by the spectacle of hearing so many young children mouthing away at words they did not understand, suggested in the late nineteenth century that the teaching of reading should be delayed until the age of eight or even 10. That definitely isn't the answer for the present day. It's as well to know

From WHERE 36 (March 1968)

what lay behind their suggestions, however, because in addition to their strong reaction against what one early writer called 'a barren action of the organs of speech upon the atmosphere', there was the idea that children would be better employed exploring their environment, extending their physical and sensory experiences, and extending their speaking vocabulary along with this extension of experience than in mouthing the usually meaningless sentences characteristic of the reading books of the day.

Today it is accepted in this country that children will begin some kind of reading experience about the age of five and that the majority of them will be able to read some simple little books by the age of seven. There are, however, some areas where 30 per cent of children who go into the junior schools have not really made a start with reading. I would say that there is something wrong with a teaching method if *while attempting to teach children to read* it fails to get the normal child on to the reading of simple sentences by the age of seven. I don't mean by that mere 'look and say' reading but actually being able to work out from the letters simply spelt words they may never have seen before, such words as occur in the following questions:

Can a dog run?
Is the sun wet?
Is an egg red?

The reason for having such a 'nonsensical' word as 'wet' after sun is to ensure that the child is actually working the word out from his letter-knowledge. If 'hot' were printed after 'sun', there is every chance that he would arrive at the right word by a simple process of association, and that would conceal something of his reading processes. Those sentences are taken from the main test in *Standard reading tests* by J. C. Daniels and myself, a test designed to find out the degree of letter-knowledge that a child possesses.

**Why can't children read?**

Now for some of the causes of failure to learn to read in the case of otherwise normal children.

**1** – A child may have been put off reading by having it thrust at him when he would rather be doing something else. It is essential that he should come to reading willing to learn. His desire to learn will be stimulated by having stories read to him and occasionally having words pointed out to him, preferably in a casual sort of way, the words being those with associations interesting to him.

**2** – Better not try to teach a child to read at all than to lose patience with him because he is slow at learning the significance of letters and at being able to work words out for himself. The nagging of an impatient mother can be a substantial cause of reading failure.

**3** – Some people will not agree with this, but experience of a number of years and hundreds of instances has convinced me that a major cause of reading backwardness is an improper use of whole-word methods. I have seen the majority of a class of six-and-a-half-year olds reading *ocvcglomc* as *aeroplane* – and this is plain ridiculous. All children at the early stages of reading guess at words, but to carry on teaching without at the same time requiring a more accurate observation of the words than outright whole-word teaching does is to encourage the child in habits of perception that will stand in his way when he moves to other books. He *must* learn what letters are for and why they are where they are in a particular order.

There are two ways of getting round the difficulties: changing the spelling to a more regular form, as is done in the initial teaching alphabet (ita), or grading the reading material, beginning with regularly spelt words like 'man', 'bus', 'animal', 'caravan' and moving gradually through the various complexities. The latter was the method adopted by J. C. Daniels and myself in the *Royal road readers*. What I am certain about is that children should be taught to read the simply spelt words at home if they are not getting them in school. Good, not harm, will come from doing so.

**Does ita work?**

Much has been written in the press and shown on television about ita but a full evaluation of this method has not yet been completed. Some parents may have no choice as to whether or not their children will be taught by this method. This creates a problem, but not an insuperable one. It is still true that words that are regularly spelt in English are nearly all unchanged in the ita versions. Therefore the parent should use those words to give the child insight into the letters, bearing in mind the points I made about this earlier and bearing in mind, too, that the child's interest must be maintained. Five or 10 minutes a day cultivating letter-knowledge with simple words can work wonders with slow learners of reading.

Have books about the house suitable for his age. Give him comics with good print design. Let him crayon and draw; that will sharpen his perceptions. Let him copy letters and words. If he wants to draw a ship, write 'ship' under it for him if he is unable to do it himself and let him copy that. Some of the cheap picture-puzzle books are very good value for the money.

If you are writing a letter to, say, his grandmother, let him draw a picture to enclose with your letter, or if he is of the age to do so, let him write a little letter. Spell out for him, or even write for him the words he cannot do himself, but encourage him as best you can to write by himself those words which because of his incipient letter-knowledge he should be able to work out for himself.

That the child should do it himself is the great thing. Teaching is not cramming or forcing; it is placing the child in the position of doing something himself and as far as the teaching of reading is concerned even the writing of little words like 'in', 'man', 'bus', and so on are steps forward.

The teaching of reading is a fascinating business; parents can help a great deal, but the greatest help comes when a parent can say as that parent wrote to me: 'We both enjoy it so much'.

*Hunter Diack was senior tutor at the Institute of Education of Nottingham University, and author of a number of books including* Reading and the psychology of perception, In spite of the alphabet, *and co-author of the* Standard reading tests *and the* Royal road readers. *He died in 1975.*

# LEARNING TO PAINT

## Janet Weinroth

AT THE ACE nursery school children can paint whenever they like. We have permanent easels on the wall, the brushes are in their places, the paint ready mixed. This is because we believe that painting is not something a child does on Tuesday afternoons or Friday mornings. It's not a 'subject' in a nursery school curriculum, but a way of expressing feelings and ideas, and a way of having fun that children need to be able to turn to just when they feel like it. It is, of course, a simple matter for a nursery school to have painting materials set up ready to be used at any moment. For mothers to provide a permanent painting corner at home is much more difficult. But if it is at all possible I advise you to do this. For if you want your children to have the chance to paint, then much the best way to arrange it is for them to choose *when* they'll paint, just as they decide *what* they'll paint.

The first problem which may occur to you is that of mess. And I know the kind of situation you have in mind. One day in the nursery two children wandered off to the paint room on their own. In two minutes flat the floor was painted with paint, all the paints were mixed up, the tables were full of paint, the chairs were full of paint and the children were full of paint. And these were children who were normally very timid. And almost every child in the nursery has some such experience, not necessarily to that extent. But they all go through the period where they dip their hands into the paint, they paint their heads, they paint their clothing. Perhaps the answer is to provide them with finger paints in the first instance, so that they can legitimately enjoy the feel of the paint and stir it about.

**A mirror of life**

As a teacher I am always being asked 'How do you get the children to do such lovely paintings? Does it just come? Do you just give them paint and brushes? The answer is that the paintings are a mirror of the child's life. He is putting on paper what he has taken in from the world around him. So if his life is rich, if he's being highly stimulated, then as a rule he will do lovely paintings. The exceptions are the children who don't choose to express themselves in this way. They prefer something else, and, for example, may spend a lot of time in the brick corner – and there's real art going on there. My experience, however, is that somehow or other painting reaches *most* children. And because it is relatively cheap to provide, and offers them so many possibilities, it is perhaps the best of the creative media to give them.

How much teaching do you need to give a young child? None at all in the sense in which you probably understand it. We make our children able to paint not by teaching them as such, but by developing their senses. Creativity exists in your child as in every child, and is simply waiting to be brought out by you or by a teacher. In the nursery the stories we read, the songs we sing, the little talks that we have (what happens to mother at home during the morning; the new baby), the games we play, the swings that we swing on, every single thing that goes on in the nursery enriches the child's ability to express himself in one form or another.

What we never do is interfere with the children in the way they express their ideas. You might think that we *owe* it to children to tell them how to do things – how to paint a house, or paint a tree. That we have a responsibility to direct their development. And in fact we are feeding them constantly, but in a subtle manner. We provide them with experiences, provoke their thought, react to the things they create, but we don't interfere. Interfering means stopping, means giving the child the feeling that you know how to draw, that he doesn't know how to draw; that *this* is the way to do it, and that's *not* the way to do it. Like saying, 'Oh, you didn't put a nose in' or 'Your man doesn't have any arms'. These are forms of interfering.

And if you want your child to show in his paintings that he has an original eye, you'll



From WHERE 29 (September 1969)

have to hold yourself back from showing him how. For it's when children have been told how to draw a house with a tree in the garden that they produce stereotypes and not the unique paintings that they'll do left to themselves.

What sort of results can you expect from your child when he first starts to paint? He will do what we call scribblings. This is true whatever age he is. Children may be in the scribbling stage when they're nearly three or turned four. If he has not had a chance to paint before, the child of four will do the exact same thing that a child of three does, or a child of two and a half does. He has to go through all the stages from the beginning. But, of course, if he starts late he may go through the early stages very quickly – in a month or two, or even a week.

When children scribble, all they are doing is extending the early kinaesthetic pleasures that they had when they just rolled their arms from one place to the other in their crib, or kicked their legs up into the air. If you give your two-year-old child a brush, he will take that brush and he will swing it back and forwards across the paper. Or he may just dab. He may swish it across the paper without even looking at what he's doing. Never expect anything from a child at this stage. Just give him the chance to paint, and lots of space. Give him the whole floor if you happen to have that kind of floor, or give him chalk and pavement outside if it's your own pavement. This is what a two and a half year old really needs. He needs just to spread his arms back and forth, and use huge crayons, large thick brushes.

**'That looks like something'**

The other day a father came into the nursery and said: 'Ah, that *looks like* something'. His child was in the scribbling period. Now I don't think there's any need at all to relate a particular scribble to anything specific. To expect anything of a child when he is in the scribbling period is as much as asking a three-month-old infant to try to walk. But there is development within the scribbling. It turns from

*A man, as painted on four consecutive occasions by a child in the ACE nursery. With each, the image becomes more complex, 'As a child grows, so does his man'.*

dabs, and uncontrolled haphazard lines, to controlled lines. At the same time we get a kind of muscular development. The larger muscles of the arm are becoming stronger, and the movements are becoming firmer and more and more controlled. In the nursery we help this with other activities. Playing on the swing and the climbing frame, running about on the tyres and balancing in the garden also work towards the development of the larger muscles, which in turn develop finer muscles.

A child who has not had the possibility of developing physically is inadequate in handling a smaller pencil or a smaller crayon. One relates to the other.

So a couple of don'ts for this stage in your child's painting are: don't ask them what they've done, and don't draw for them. On the positive side, do provide them with the possibility of working on a large scale, and encourage their physical growth in other ways. And finally watch how their scribbles develop. Be concerned if the child is doing the same thing over and over again. If he is, it's a danger sign. Children are dynamic creatures. Their bodies are changing at an enormous rate. And if they do the same thing every day, I tend to worry about it. Of course, a child will repeat something for a limited period, but that's merely practising until he gains confidence. But if this goes on for a very long time, it looks as though the child is afraid to move on. This may signal to you some emotional problem he has. Certainly if he's at a nursery school it's worth mentioning it to his teacher so that she can relate it to how well he is coping with all the other children there.

The next stage is 'the naming of the scribbling' period. This is fascinating because we get very interesting comments from the children on what they've done. The naming is quite involuntary. We don't ask 'what's that?' but a child will come up with a painting and say 'that's a crocodile' or 'it is a kind of animal with no legs'. For it's at this stage that a child begins to connect the lines that he draws with the things that he sees around him. He recognises 'a crocodile' in what his hands have accidentally created. He might never paint another crocodile, and I would be very careful about urging him to do so. It is enough that his observation has developed so that he achieves the recognition. It is not only shapes that suggest names to the children: it may be the colours they have put together. So that a painting with lots of colour but very little form will be 'mummy at the seaside' or 'a sunny day' or 'that's Cambridge like it is now'. The most important thing at this stage is to try to be on the spot to share the child's pleasure in this recognition, and to write down what he says word for word. The blobs may seem like nothing to you until the child talks about it. Like Edmund: 'this is so horrible that I am going to whisper it to you. It is a dragon machine, and it makes dragons come out'.

**Did he plan his painting?**

At this stage you can never be sure how far a child deliberately sets out to make a train, say, or whether it came out incidentally and so he added the smoke to confirm the impression.

It is now that certain basic formations tend to crop up repeatedly: they all spring from the vertical line, the horizontal line, the joining of the two, the circle. What happens is that these very simple elements can be spontaneously combined to make rain, snakes, a road, a ladder, a spider, a wheel, a flower, the sun. These are the images that occur. Going on from this it is easy to see why children choose 'man' as a theme so early in their painting – in the first stages just a circle and two vertical lines. But children need practice before they get to this point. The link between the circle and the line demands a great deal of control.

The first time your child draws a man it may be just a circle for the head with perhaps a mouth and two eyes, and the legs coming straight out of it. The second time he may add arms as well. As the child grows so does his man. Later he adds ears and hair, and gives him a body of some sort. And he will be making a tremendous step forward when he gives him ground as well to stand on.

**The face means most**

The most important thing to the child is the face, and the face is huge. The body may be no more than a stump. The proportions will be way out of what we as adults would consider correct. But, in fact, it is not out of proportion in relation to how they see us. It is our faces that make the greatest impression on them. They watch our mouths, they watch our eyes, they listen to us talk a lot more than adults do. They're very aware of every movement we make in our faces. As the child grows older his man becomes more in proportion to what we accept as normal. It is taller. The arms come right out of the shoulders. The body is in two pieces. The legs may be clothed in trousers or a skirt. The child becomes much more concerned with detail. We get a man with hands. At the age of four they don't usually count the fingers. There may be as many as ten. But a bit later the child gets very concerned with how many fingers.

Finally, the child may relate the figure to his surroundings, as Matthew did when he drew 'mummy and the television box'.

Since the concept of shelter is very important to a child, another basic theme is the house. Yet though all the children in the nursery may paint houses, not one resembles another. There will be an odd chimney in one, a slanting roof in another, a round door, French windows. But that is only if the child hasn't been told: 'this is the way we draw a house'.

Generally speaking, children reach this stage during their fourth year, that is if they've been working through the different stages from the age of three. And from the house he moves to the larger environment. If his trip to the seashore has affected him, he may paint 'the ship in the deep sea'. His particular surroundings provide him with subjects so that one child who lived in the country liked to paint tractors. One had 'a bucket on the front and a digger arm at the rear'. For this is a period of very keen observation. One child in the nursery did a painting of 'a see-saw with two people' in which the nearer child is larger, and the child who is further away smaller. It would be difficult to say whether or not she intended that, but it indicates a very keen eye.

At four and a half a child will use painting as an outlet for his growing appreciation of situations and as part of his growing fluency in making stories. As an example of the first we get 'this is a camel and he's running very fast because there's an elephant behind him with water in his trunk'. And for the second we have Edmund's 'fish story' which he told in six paintings:

1 – 'here are roaring giant fishes'
2 – 'this is a man with a fishing tackle fishing in the sea'
3 – 'another fishing tackle'
4 – 'sea with only the fish'
5 – 'only the sea itself'
6 – 'another man with fishing tackle, but he hasn't got to the sea as yet'.

The child at the end of his nursery school life will be beginning to take an interest in reading and number, and this will show in his painting. He will experiment with letters of his own accord, drawing them backwards, the right way, sideways or upside down. If you take the analogy of learning to drive at 30, say, you will understand how something which can be explained very simply must be practised over and over again before we can master it. So it is with the children making patterns out of some of the letters in their name. In time, they'll write them the accepted way by themselves, so we don't interfere by correcting them in the meantime. As with letters so with numbers. These will crop up naturally in the work the older children in the nursery do, like Harold's 'this is a bird with three hats on him, and he is standing on one leg' or Edmund's 'this is a camel with four humps', 'a camel with seven humps', 'a camel with eight humps', 'a camel with 10 humps'. Most children of this age can count easily enough, but to match each number to one of the things being counted is a real achievement. A final characteristic of the child's work just before he goes to school is experimentation with design and colour. After a child has had some practice in combining lines and colours, she may then incorporate what she has learnt in giving the little girl she is painting a plaid skirt. At about this time children will be using table games to make patterns as well, and all these kinds of experience will help them when they next pick up a paintbrush. All the experiences and events in the busy life of a pre-school child will give him material for his paintings.

You can provide children with all the equipment you like – the best of paint brushes, the largest sheets of paper – but if you do not give them intellectual and emotional stimulation, they will paint very dull and uninteresting pictures. Their paintings reflect the world that we create for them.

*Janet Weinroth was director of the ACE nursery school from 1966 to 1968.*

# CHILDREN WHO LEARN TO READ BEFORE GOING TO SCHOOL

Christopher Jarman

*A grandfather writes:*

'My daughter had to bring her boy and live with us when he was about one year old. As soon as he could talk I tried to interest him in toys, play things and so on, that had some educational value. I have no teaching qualifications whatever. I was until recently a newsagent/tobacconist.

At that time it was my practice to have a second breakfast at about 9.30 and during that half-hour or so I taught him the alphabet and the sound of each letter in the same way I was taught 66 years ago. I taught him the figures; got him writing and drawing. Bought him, as I say, blackboards with lines of beads to count, big clock faces, ABC bricks and particularly ABC books. Later I got him special educational books.

I don't thing he was any sharper than my other four grandsons. I believe what I did for him would have had the same result with them. Looking back I seem to think it was really easy, done in play (no question of cramming) with education in mind.

He could tell the time when he was three and read children's picture books, and at four he found the TV programmes for his grandmother.

He was reading daily papers when he went to school and then it seemed he had to go through all the motions, being shown a postcard of a cow and so on to learn their way how to read. He would come home from school frustrated, having to sit listening for hours alongside children who couldn't read, or write, with the school's way of teaching until they were eight or nine. He had to mark time for two or three years. I feel he was held back at the time at this village primary school. Nevertheless he passed 11-plus, was top pupil of the year, winning the school shield.

I believe that reading is the gateway to everything, the most important item of all and if I had my time over again I should start teaching my children to read as soon as they could talk.'

**Sunday paper survey**

This letter was sent to me as a result of a request which was printed in *The News of the World* which asked parents who had taught their children to read before five to contact me. I got 150 letters in all from such parents; a quarter of them had taught more than one child to read. This is a report of what they had to say.

Of course, I am not able to apply any check that the children concerned could objectively be said to be reading. The books and methods used in the families naturally varied considerably. However, the internal evidence of nearly all the letters is detailed and convincing, particularly in the indirect comments made by the writers. For example, one mother wrote that 'when our daughter went to primary school at seven, the only complaint was that she was too far advanced in her studies for her age'. This parent had taught her daughter herself, as the family was living abroad until that time.

Most parents seemed to consider that their child could read when they no longer confined themselves to formal readers or the 'kit', but could tackle anything they wished to read.

An accidental but most useful aspect of the inquiry was that it became evident that the majority of the people writing to me did not understand that this was an educational inquiry, as such. They assumed that I was a parent who wanted advice on how to teach my own child to read. This attitude is evident from the tone of many letters and gives their evidence an authentic ring. Thus they were not making points about any educational success they had scored, but simply relating their experience:

> At two I wrote him single words on cards in large writing. These were of everyday things that interested him – car, biscuit and drink. He said the words when shown the cards but I was not sure if he really knew them. I therefore decided to wait until he was older, as I thought he was not yet ready.

A number of interesting facts emerge from the letters, although the opinions themselves are perhaps the most illuminating.

First of all, the backgrounds of the parents seem to be representative of all social classes. In general conversation with teachers it is easy to get the impression that to actively encourage one's child to read is a purely middle-class aim. Out of 150 *News of the World* readers, only about 36 could be placed in the professional or managerial range. Thus nearly 75 per cent of the parents were in clerical or unskilled manual occupations. It is evident, therefore, that in a minority of working-class homes there is active pre-school help in reading given by mothers.

The impression gained through reading some of the letters, however, is that mothers have been made to feel guilty about this. One says the subject is 'taboo'; another, the wife of a fitter in Catford, wrote that:

> the doctor at the clinic advised me not to teach him (age four and a half) as it was wrong for him. I just let him pick a book or two at the library such as *Ant & Bee*, also *Jane and Peter* and a couple of *Dr. Seuss* books. At the moment he is reading *Janet and John* Book Four. Had the doctor advised otherwise I am sure he would be much more advanced, but I took her advice and tried not to push him.

One feels that the general sensitivity and intelligence of many working-class mothers is grossly underestimated by both teachers and doctors. The main reason given by

From WHERE 57 (May 1971)

teachers for discouraging parents from teaching young children is to protect the child from being 'pushed'. The evidence in these letters is consistent with the normal principle in law that the parent is in general the best protector of the child, and needs encouragement, not inhibition.

**How they did it**

It is very interesting to see how parents describe the methods they have used. In most cases the parents have learnt to use the near technical terms 'look and say' or 'phonic' to describe what they did. In some letters, however, it is possible only to infer what method was used – either from what the mother says, or from the books or apparatus she used. For example, where a mother states that her daughter, aged three, can pick out the letters of the alphabet which she has printed on the wall for her, the method used has been noted as 'alphabetic'. Where a mother writes, 'I taught her by sounds', the method has been noted as 'phonic'. It is obvious, however, from the detailed contents of letters, that parents, like good infant teachers, vary their methods from time to time.

'Look and say' approaches seem to dominate the parents' teaching nevertheless, and from the letters one would conclude that the parents' sensitivity to the abilities and reactions of their own children has caused this. Where an assessment has been possible the approaches were:

| | |
|---|---|
| look and say | – 96 replies |
| alphabetic | – 35 replies |
| phonic | – 9 replies |

The high proportion of alphabetic approaches is extremely interesting, in view of its almost total disappearance from schools. However, historically it is, of course, the oldest method of teaching reading. I believe that, as with early phonic teaching, children may indeed appear to be *taught* by these methods but with certain exceptions the child *learns* through look-and-say, even though the adult may not always be aware of it. With the close and loving relationship of a mother added to the operation, the experience of alphabetical analysis, together with the child's interest, may have a highly beneficial effect on later learning and spelling.

The success of these parents is without doubt due to the fact that they knew their own children's interests and fostered them. They were sensitive to their own child's needs and capacities. Many mothers of four year olds felt that their child was ready for school and that a reading session of perhaps only 15 minutes a day was a great satisfaction to them both.

**Books and materials**

Nearly all the letters mentioned by name either the books or schemes parents had used to help their children – in some cases commercially published reading kits such as the cards produced by Waddington's. Many parents had made large flash cards such as infant school teachers often use, or had made their own kit from instructions in Glen Doman's book, *Teach Your Baby to Read* (Jonathan Cape, 1963). By far the most popular books were from the Ladybird series. In fact 71 letters specifically mentioned these, although not all had followed their Key Words Scheme. Some parents just bought the easiest books and used them in conjunction with home-made cards or other simple readers. The parents who had used the Key Words system were able to check their child's progress more accurately by stating, for example, 'at four and a half he is now reading book 5A'.

The next most frequently used system was Glen Doman's kit. Altogether 22 letters mention his book or apparatus in some form. Some of these parents felt that they had started too early, and broke off teaching at two to two and a half years old and waited until later. For example, a ladies' hairdresser from London wrote:

I started teaching my daughter to read at the age of two, by the method of holding up a printed word, with the aid of a book called, *Teach Your Baby to Read.* By the age of two years three months, she could recognise 17 words. But realising the attention and admiration she was achieving, an uncontrollable sense of humour came into her 'lessons' and she would say the wrong word every time, laughing and waiting for everybody else to laugh. I discontinued this method.

At about the age of three and a half I started to teach her to write the alphabet, this she quickly learned.

At the age of four I bought three books. *The Ladybird Key Words Reading Scheme* 1a, 1b and 1c. In three days, Amber could read the first book from cover to cover. Then the second one was learned as easily.

This mother's letter is one of several who decided to stop teaching for a year or more and try again later. The rapid progress made at the *second attempt* is typical of this kind of approach. The earlier experience may well be a cause of this. Several experiments of this nature, notably McManus (1961) and those described by Lynn (1963) support the idea of early training leading to later more rapid learning. A useful simple survey of the most recent opinion can be found in the Ladybird book, *Teaching Reading* by W. Murray (1969).

A small number of parents had bought and used a school reading scheme, the most popular being *Janet and John*. There appear to be two quite conflicting reasons given for buying school reading scheme books for use at home. One parent says that she bought the same scheme as is used in the infant school to which the child is destined to go. Another parent says that she bought a particular reader deliberately because it was not used at the infant school, and thought it best to widen her child's experience.

No parent gave any indication that she understood that certain books were biased towards certain approaches to teaching. For example, *Janet and John* and *Queensway* are basically look and say orientated. *Gay Way* and *Beacon Readers* are based on the story method, *Gay Way* with a particularly phonic bias.

Nevertheless, the choice of books appears to be largely irrelevant, compared with the care, patience, adaptability and interest shown by the parents. For example, the housewife (an ex-shop assistant) who had started her daughter off on *Gay Way Red Book* and *Old Lob Book One* at age four wrote:

You may be interested to know that my daughter, now aged six years one month, started going to school at five years and this week had a reading test at school based on the Ladybird *Learning to Read* books and was found to have a reading age of nine and a half to 10 years.

No parents in the survey had attempted to use ita, although one or two said that they had wondered what it was, or that their own child had gone to an infant school where ita was used. One mother of five children in Kent wrote of her eldest daughter's experience with ita:

I started teaching the eight year old to read when she was four, not knowing what form of reading the school practised. I just taught her words like 'cat', 'dog', 'mat', 'baby' and so on, which she memorised very well, and even proceeded to write very well after about six weeks. When she started school at five years of age, she was put on the Initial Teaching Alphabet books, which I thought she would find very confusing. But she progressed very well indeed and was put on the *Janet and John* ordinary reading series at five and a half years, when she was already way ahead of her classmates.

Another mother, who had been a typist with nine O levels before having three children, taught her son, Keith, to read at four, then found that his infant school used ita:

My son Keith was nearly four years old when he received, at my request, the first three books in the Ladybird series of reading books (*ie* 1a, 2a, 3a). We definitely did not have specific reading sessions with these books, but as all children's books in our home are always kept readily accessible, they were frequently looked through and used by talking about the pictures they contain.

It was easily a year later that I realised that he was actually reading these three books – I did not think there was anything particularly unusual about this – I had no experience of other children's reading abilities and thought that all children could read something before they started school. When he could read all 3a I bought the next book in the series and from then on we did have sit-down periods of reading. I listened and corrected where necessary; I did find that with most new words they could be repeated endless times on one day and they would not stay in his memory but as soon as he saw them the next day he would recognise them. I only bought the 'a' books in the series as he went through them without difficulty, and by the time he was due to start school in April he was on to 7a.

At that time our village school taught reading by the ita method and of course I felt this would be useless to Keith (by then I had realised he was fairly advanced for his age with his reading). I had a little difficulty in persuading his new headmistress that he could actually read, but in the end she gave him a test and assured me he would not start the ita method at all. Keith will be six in March this year and is still very much in advance of his age where reading is concerned.

It would seem here that if a child has really learnt to read and the school is made fully aware of this, it makes very little difference whether the infant classes use ita or not.

Altogether 198 children in this survey had been taught to read by their parents before starting school. The numbers of boys and girls were about equal, 104 girls and 94 boys. Three of the children were adopted. Most had been started on word recognition between the ages of one and a half and four, and most were reading by between three years 10 months and five and a half.

There seems little doubt that this particular province of education, far from being a skill best left to trained teachers, is one where the close *one-to-one relationship of parent and child often outweighs the theoretical knowledge held by some teachers.* It is true, of course, that when teachers are trained to teach reading they are expected to think in terms of work with large classes. This means that the encouragement of extremely rapid progress which is sometimes

L. L. Fahidy

desirable – for example, three books in three days – is often quite foreign to the infant teacher. Whereas the parent with no preconceptions will be able to follow a quick child's lead more easily.

There is no evidence in this survey, either direct or indirect, which suggests that the parents' effort have ever been a positive hindrance to the child. One or two mothers did say that they sometimes regretted taking a child so far ahead of his contemporaries as he had become bored at school due to being underestimated. This is a slight risk, but one which could surely be overcome by closer consultation between home and school.

All recent reports and surveys on early learning in children have stressed the importance of parental help and encouragement. Only very short-sighted and prejudiced teachers are unreasonable about such parental involvement. Most infant teachers with classes of 30 or 40 children will bless the mother who has already taught her child to read. There are so many other interesting and worthwhile things the school can provide once this first hurdle has been painlessly passed.

Parents essentially have their own children's interests at heart. The destructively over-ambitious mother exists, but the number of parents like this is extremely small. Why is it that the 'experts' seem to believe that only *they* care for the children, and that parents are only waiting to exploit theirs?

*Christopher Jarman is a primary school adviser with Oxfordshire county council.*

# 2 The state of play

Alan H. Robson

# PRE-SCHOOL EDUCATION 1: STATE PROVISION

Pamela McKeown

**What does the state set out to provide? What is the thinking behind that provision? We present a factual guide.**

TO CELEBRATE THE centenary of state education an exhibition *Learning for a purpose* was set up and toured the country in 1970. In the accompanying booklet a nursery school was defined as a place which 'sets out to provide a world which starts the senses tingling, fires the imagination and opens up vast areas of experience' and offers opportunity 'by invitation to learn'.

The maintained schools – the primary schools, nursery schools, and nursery classes – are staffed by trained teachers or nursery nurses. The ratio is better than that offered to children of compulsory school age – *ie* children are entitled to a place in an infant or all-age primary school (five to 11 years) the term after their fifth birthday. Approximately 10 per cent of pre-school children are catered for in maintained nursery schools and nursery classes but the provision is uneven throughout England and Wales.

To give an example of 'average provision', before local government re-organisation in April 1974, Bristol LEA had approximately 2,000 nursery places. Some city and county local education authorities would have more, some less or even none. (See *LEA league table on the expansion of nursery places* WHERE 87)

## Nursery schools and classes

*A nursery school* receives children between two-and-a-half and five years old and is staffed with a three-year trained teacher for every 20 children, who would be qualified to teach nursery and infant children, and a nursery nurse who has two years training leading to the Nursery Nurse Examination Board (NNEB) certificate. It is a separate school in its own right, with its own head-teacher. All teachers are paid on the Burnham scale.

*A nursery class* receives children between the ages of three and five, is staffed by similarly trained teachers and nursery nurses but may have as many as 30 children. It is attached to an infant or all-age primary school and often housed in a similar classroom to the others in the school; though it should have its own separate outdoor play area.

The Department of Education and Science recommends that each child should have 25 sq ft of indoor play space and 100 sq ft of outdoor play space of which 40 sq ft should be paved – some of which is preferably roofed over.

The ideal environment and daily programme are planned with very young children in mind, and the aim is all-round development – physical, intellectual, social, emotional, aesthetic, moral and so on. Great care is taken in the admission process – and parents (especially mothers) are expected to stay with their children until such time as they are well settled and willing to stay on their own. In a typical school or class mid-morning and afternoon snacks are provided, usually milk or orange juice, raw fruit and so on, plus a carefully planned midday dinner served in an intimate, civilised manner. Individual beds are available for all children who need or want to rest. The children are encouraged to become independent and the staff stimulate language development in both a one-to-one situation and groups.

In general, all the usual raw materials are available – water, wet and dry sand, clay, wood and a variety of creative materials such as paint, chalk, crayon, waste materials for model building; cooking takes place and many children are interested in doll and puppet-making. Big apparatus is available indoors and out for climbing, pushing and pulling, plus hideaway areas, which invite imitative play such as home corners stocked with small size domestic articles, dressing up clothes and a multitude of dolls and their 'properties' such as prams and beds. Books and music may have special areas devoted to them. Stories are told and read and children left free as to whether they join a group or not. Parents should be made welcome in the playrooms and staff should free themselves so as to be able to discuss the children and their needs, especially at the beginning and end of each session.

Local education authorities have complete freedom to organise nursery schools and nursery classes so that children may be offered either full-time or part-time (usually half day) places. The demand for places far outstrips provision and this usually results in priority being given to children in particular need. This may be one or more of:

- ☐ any form of handicap
- ☐ unsuitable or overcrowded housing
- ☐ broken homes or single parent families
- ☐ physical or emotional need of mother and/or child
- ☐ inadequate nurture due to poverty or inadequate parental care
- ☐ late or faulty language development.

Under the recommendations of the White Paper *Education: A framework for expansion* (HMSO December 1972, 31½p), it is envisaged that by 1982 increased provision will result in nursery education being

*Pages 20/21:* Dona Haycraft

From WHERE 100 (January 1975)

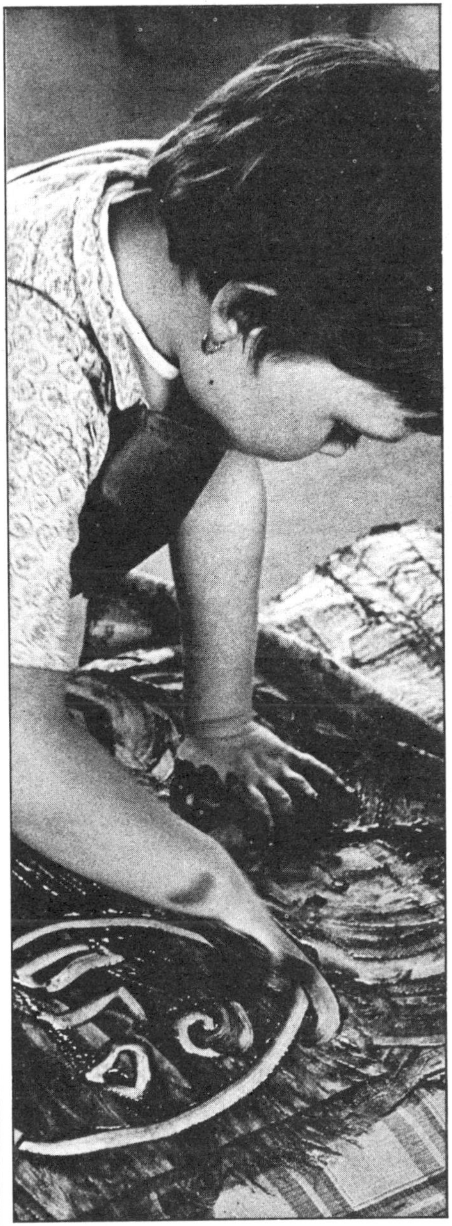

available to children, whose parents wish it, to the level recommended in the Plowden report of 1967 – *ie* part-time for 90 per cent of four year olds and 50 per cent of three year olds.

Many people like myself believe this is quite inadequate. The ratio has been set at one adult to 13 children (*ie* groups of 26 staffed by a teacher and a nursery nurse) for reasons of economy. The practice is also common of making all places part-time so that 26 children would attend in the morning and a different 26 in the afternoon. Certainly this results in more children receiving nursery education, and the heads of some nursery schools and classes have even gone as far as to offer places to children for only one term in an effort to reduce their waiting list.

In my view this is a mistake and reduces the overall value of nursery education. Many children cannot adjust quickly enough to get full benefit from a short day. Equally important, the opportunity for a balanced midday meal and a rest (if required) is lost, and progressive play (just as vital) is not possible. In a more leisurely day, powers of concentration and perseverance can develop, investigation can be more prolonged and detailed (cause and effect understood) as can the intellectual stimulus and language development which results from skilled adult stimulus and participation. Younger and older children learn much from each other socially and intellectually.

Finally, the strain on the staff can become acute with twice daily preparation of the environment and double the number of children and parents to whom to relate. Nursery schools and nursery classes do not seek to replace homes, but to supplement and complement them. Experience has shown that parents often become more effective and responsible as a result of their children attending nursery schools and nursery classes.

As nursery schools and nursery classes are part of maintained primary education there are no fees, except for dinner charges. Some children will be entitled to free meals. Attendance is for the same hours and weeks as primary schools.

Unfortunately there is a serious shortage of nursery staff and some local education authorities are compelled to employ unqualified personnel. Nursery schools tend to be small (in Bristol between 33 to 120 children) and this reduces career prospects, as scale posts are few and far between. It is hoped that if nursery classes are attached to schools in units of two or more that more nursery trained teachers will be able to look for promotion within the pre-school age range.

**Day nurseries and nursery centres**

These used to be the responsibility of the health authority but since August 1972 have been the concern of the social services. Nationally the available provision is approximately eight places per 1,000 children under five years. Places in day nurseries are only available to children whose parents cannot care for them, either temporarily or long term. Babies can be accepted from three months – but this is considered more as a last resort than desirable. Places are allocated by the central office and once again demand far outstrips the places available.

The day nursery is usually open from 8 a.m. to 5.30 or 6 p.m., Monday to Friday the year round, except for bank holidays. At present the staffing ratio is one adult to five children – but a recommendation in 1972 was that it should be improved to 1 : 4. The cost to the parent varies from 5p to £1 per day – according to ability to pay. The matron and senior members of staff are usually SRN or NNEB trained. During training all nursery nurses cover the period from birth to seven years of child development, but specialise either from birth to three, or five to seven years. Normally nursery nurses in schools tend to choose the older age span, while nursery nurses in day nurseries prefer the younger age range.

There has always been a very high standard of hygiene and physical care and nowadays an increasing interest in language and intellectual development. In all three types of nursery provision, close attention is paid to health and regular medical inspections take place, which parents can and should be encouraged to attend.

The rate of pay for NNEB-trained staff compares unfavourably with many unskilled jobs, and it is increasingly difficult

Nick Skinner

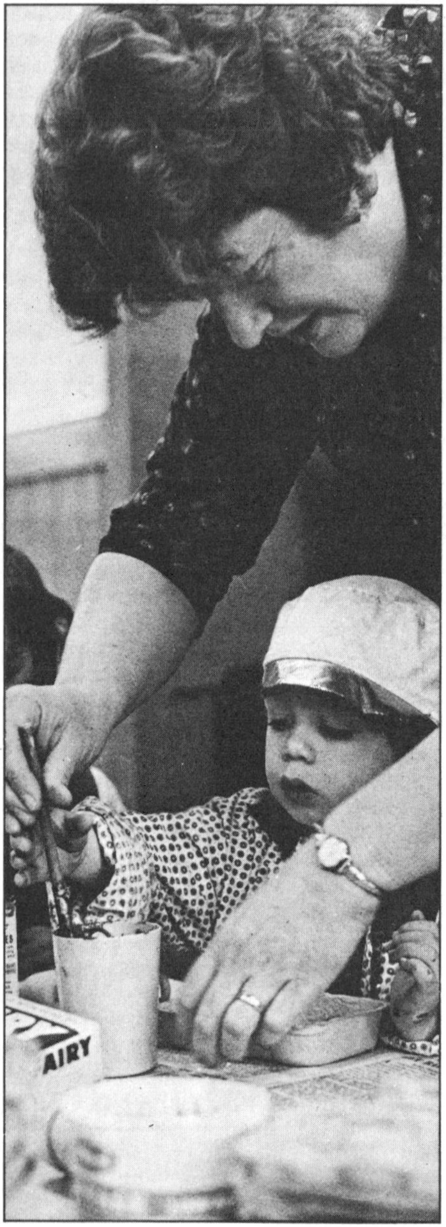

for nursery nurses (however highly motivated) to remain in their chosen profession.

There are a handful of nursery centres functioning. They are an experimental attempt to offer a more flexible provision by combining day nurseries and nursery schools under one roof. The intention was to make it possible to meet individual needs and allow for transfer from one type of provision to the other. Unfortunately the fact that the Education Service and Social Services are totally different financial organisations, implement different job specifications and have very differing requirements for buildings and equipment, has led to every sort of problem. Solutions are hard to find despite good will on both sides and warm co-operation between staff in the nurseries and the officers of both services.

With local politicians controlling the committees responsible for the running of the education service and social services, this can lead to decisions which make full integration impossible. The headteacher is responsible to the education committee while the matron likewise is answerable to the social service committee. Similarly the Department of Education and Science and the Department of Health and Social Security are separate bodies. The situation is further complicated by the fact that the Social Services license playgroups under the Childminders Act of 1968, whereas formerly they were the responsibility of local education authorities. Some local education authorities now have playgroups running in vacant classrooms in primary schools and many of them offer training courses to playgroup personnel, staffed chiefly by advisers, teachers and nursery nurse course tutors.

*Pamela McKeown is senior advisor for nursery and infant education for Avon county.*

## bookbox

*Our young children* (HMSO, 1969, 17½p)
*Play with a purpose for under-sevens,* by E. Matterson (Penguin, 75p)
*The nursery years* by Susan Isaacs (Routledge, 90p)
*Pre-school education,* the report of the Schools Council project on pre-school education by Marianne Parry and Hilda Archer (Macmillan, £3.95)

# PRE-SCHOOL EDUCATION 2: PLAYGROUPS

Brenda Crowe

**Just what is involved in deciding not just between nursery school and playgroup, but playgroup and playgroup? If the choice is there how do you make up your mind? This article explains.**

THE PUBLICITY GIVEN to the growing awareness of the importance of the first five years in a child's life is, in some ways, a mixed blessing. Certainly it was time that the needs of the under-fives were highlighted, but hundreds of thousands of anxious parents are now frantically trying to find this highly desirable pre-school education for their children – and it isn't available to most of them.

Commerce has been quick to latch on to this newly aroused concern of parents to help their children more specifically before school. Teaching toys, kits and books abound – some good, some poor, some counter-productive. But even the good ones are wide open to being misunderstood and misinterpreted to the detriment of the one thing that matters above all, the parent-child relationship.

In view of all the current pressures it

From WHERE 100 (January 1975)

is time to reassure parents that even if they live in an area where there is no pre-school provision of any kind, there is still no need to feel that their children's start in life has inevitably been jeopardised. Many parents can and do provide love, security, a warm bond of communication heightened by conversation, a rich play experience, a rich home-making experience, opportunities to play with other children of similar ages (and different stages), friendly adults who will help to lessen the child's intense dependence on the parent-child relationship, and an ever increasing contact with the community and the experiences it holds.

**What is play?**

It is also time for all of us to ask ourselves what we are doing to the word 'play'. To polarise play as being either 'educational' or 'occupational' is to miss the spontaneity, the joy, the healing, the integrating force, and the mystery at the heart of the experience of play. If, through popular misconception, we try to 'use' play as a means of getting children ready for school and higher education we shall end up by robbing children of their childhood, upon which the foundations of the quality of their adult life is so heavily dependent. It is important that parents understand the value of play, but also that they don't forget what they felt like when, as children, they said at the end of every meal 'can I go and play?'. Escape to freedom and bliss!

**How do you choose?**

The previous article by Pamela McKeown explains the various forms of state provision, and this one is a guide to the very varied playgroup provision spreading over the country: over 7,000 playgroups belonging to the Pre-school Playgroups Association (PPA), with 700 new ones joining every year, and many running independently.

Playgroups, playschools, nursery schools, nursery groups – alas, the name will tell you nothing – and the term 'nursery school' can be particularly misleading, so check any such establishments against the requirements of a state nursery school. It may be that you still feel it is right for your child, but it is tragic that so many parents without the confidence or knowledge to judge for themselves pay for what they assume must be 'the best', and sometimes never discover that it offered neither the benefits of a state nursery school nor a good playgroup.

The common factors are that the premises and the person responsible for the venture have been passed by the Social Services department in accordance with the Nurseries and Childminders Regulation Act, 1948; the minimum ratio of children to staff varies between 8:1 and 10:1 and, in some areas, the groups will not have been allowed to start unless the playgroup leader is 'suitably qualified'.

What is a 'suitable qualification'? What is a playgroup? Until one understands the nature of the latter it isn't possible to answer the former question. The ethos of the playgroup movement has evolved from the experience of those working in widely different areas, and it may be helpful to trace the development over the last fourteen years.

**Development**

In 1961 the first playgroups were an attempt to provide the closest possible imitation of nursery schools until such time as there should be universal state nursery school provision. The mothers joined together to find premises to rent for two or three hours a few times a week; they tried to find

Henry Grant

teachers who would lead the venture in return for a token payment, and the charge to the children was kept to the sum that would just cover these two expenses. Fund-raising activities provided the money for equipment and play materials, and the mothers took it in turn to be the teachers' voluntary helpers.

As they grew more enthusiastic, the helpers asked for playgroup courses. These playgroup courses are now inextricably part of the playgroup movement, and a nationally recognised series of courses is developing. The combination of playing with children, attending classes to learn how better to provide for their play, going back to the children to put into practice what they had learnt, and returning to the classes yet again to question and discuss, proved to be a dynamic growth point for everyone concerned.

Another revelation was the improvement in the health and happiness (how closely connected they are!) of the mothers involved. They saw their child with other children, and anxieties slipped into perspective. They compared notes with each other, and were comforted to find that a great many mothers fear that they too are 'going round the bend' for up to two years after childbirth. They were surprised that others had quick-silver toddlers who demanded such constant vigilance that a few moments of peace and privacy was an impossible luxury even in the lavatory.

Roger Mayne

**Growing up**

As happiness, experience, knowledge, and understanding grew, so did abilities. People found themselves doing things, making things, and shouldering responsibilities that revealed a potential that they had no idea they possessed. The mother involvement that started as an economic necessity was suddenly seen to be immensely rewarding and important.

This knowledge brought new insight – the 'suitably qualified' playgroup leader had to be someone who could relate to children in front of the mothers and their neighbours in such a way that the mother's self-esteem was heightened, not diminished. She had to be able to encourage the learning and confidence of the mothers as well as the children; she had to make the mothers feel as important, wanted, needed and appreciated as the children. And all the time she had to hold the balance so that both children and parents benefited to the maximum but to the detriment of neither. Given this, the learning flowed back into the homes to benefit the playgroup child, the younger siblings and the relationship with the older children.

By 1973 PPA had to re-define its aims to 'PPA exists to help parents to understand and to provide for the needs of their young children. It aims to promote community situations in which parents can, with growing enjoyment and confidence, make the best uses of their own knowledge and resources in the development of their children and themselves.'

Henry Grant

## Playgroups and rising rents

*Brenda Crowe reports* In some areas the rents have gone up from £1 to £4 per session. We are still gathering information, but it is clear that oil heating has raised the costs particularly. Some playgroups have raised money to install meters for electric heating, and have proved that the new rate was not the true cost of heating.

We know some groups have closed, but not how many. Often the playgroup is the only group to pay rent, and Brownies, women's groups and so on enjoy the residual heat in the afternoon that has been paid for by the playgroup.

By no means do all playgroups belong to PPA, nor are they all committed to the idea of parent-involvement; or, if they are, not all are yet able to put their ideals into practice. Only you will know what sort of playgroups you have in your vicinity. If you don't happen to like what you know, it would be a pity to condemn the particular playgroups together with the whole playgroup movement, the potential of which is so much greater than the sum total of its playgroups.

**Fact finding**

A survey carried out by PPA at the end of 1973 produced a definitive picture of the playgroup development:

☐ there were a quarter of a million children in PPA playgroups

☐ their parents were paying just over £5 million a year in fees

☐ one in six playgroups received a grant (40% of all grants come from Social Services, and 28% from Education, most of which went to provide free places for needy children)

☐ most playgroups also provide free places once they have covered the cost of the initial outlay on equipment

☐ 63% of playgroups had a rota system of mother helpers (there are nearly 50,000 mother helpers working in playgroups)

☐ 74% of all playgroups involved parents in administration, or working alongside the children, or both

☐ the average number of children was 24 per session

☐ the average fee was 22p

☐ the average token payment for playgroup leaders was £1 to £1·50, with 50p to 75p for the one regular assistant

☐ there were over 24,000 regular staff in addition to the mother helpers

☐ the rents were around 75p to £1·75 (there is a crippling increase this year that will force the closure of some groups *see box above ie 1975*)

☐ 25% of all playgroups were in villages

☐ 69% of the playgroups had at least one member of staff who had attended playgroup courses.

A nationally recognised pattern of playgroups was beginning to emerge.

**On equal footing**

Many parents, from every type of community, have made it crystal clear that they want to be involved in the early education of their children. They don't want the job done for them, they want to be helped to do it together for their own children – and they want the 'experts' to offer help in such a way that cultural roots are not severed, nor loyalties to parents and in-laws strained. The balance between the total needs of children, and the growing ability of their parents to meet these needs is vital and delicate – hence the importance of linking playgroups and playgroup courses, and of preparing tutors specifically for this work.

Some of us so-called experts have been humbled to see how gifted, capable and wise so-called uneducated parents are with the children in their own communities. Some of us have been shamed to look back and see that in the early days of our playgroup tutoring we tried to 'make them like us' instead of helping them to be more fully themselves. All of us have been staggered by the enthusiasm and aptitude for learning of parents everywhere. All of us have been shocked to discover the extent of loneliness, guilt, frustration and anxiety that lurks behind the bright and cheerful public faces of so many of the mothers of the under-fives.

Whatever you decide to do, never place a child anywhere without a visit to ascertain that there is a wide range of activities and materials; an atmosphere of happiness, busyness and security; a willingness for you to stay for as long as your child needs you; and a welcome for you that is as warm as the welcome for him. Finally, since everyone who works with children gives her 'feel' to the group, you will need to sense for yourself whether or not your particular child is likely to be happy in that particular environment.

*Brenda Crowe is national adviser to the Pre-school Playgroups Association.*

## bookbox

*The playgroup movement* by Brenda Crowe (Allen and Unwin £2·75)
*The Penguin book of playgroups* by Joyce Lucas and Vivienne McKennell (Penguin 80p)
Three publications available from the PPA, Alford House, Aveline Street, London SE11 5DJ or 7 Royal Terrace, Glasgow G3 7NT (all prices include postage):
*Parents in playgroup* (15p); *Playgroup activities* (60p); *The importance of playgroups in education and the social services* (45p).

Henry Grant

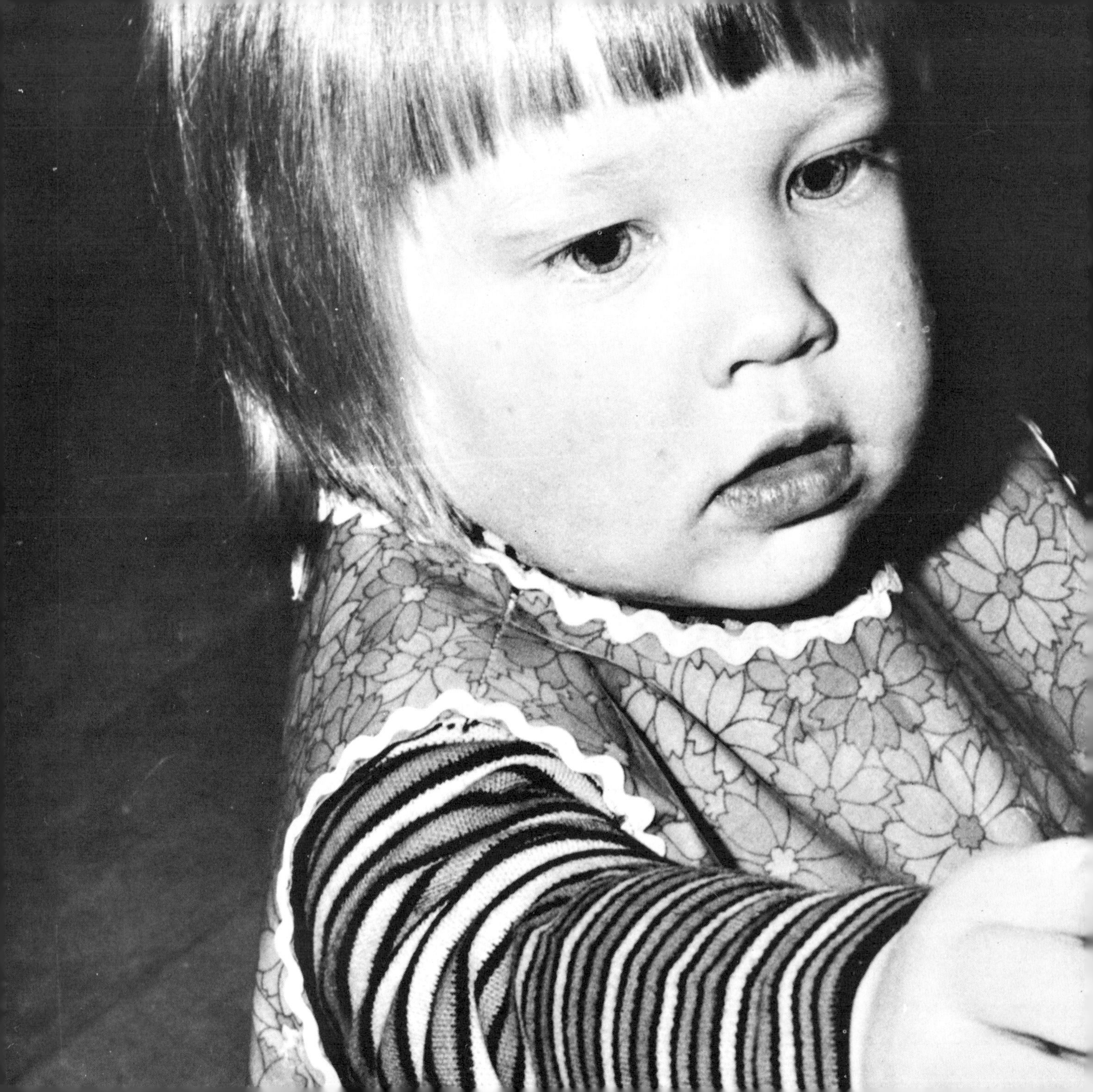

# 3 Know how for parents

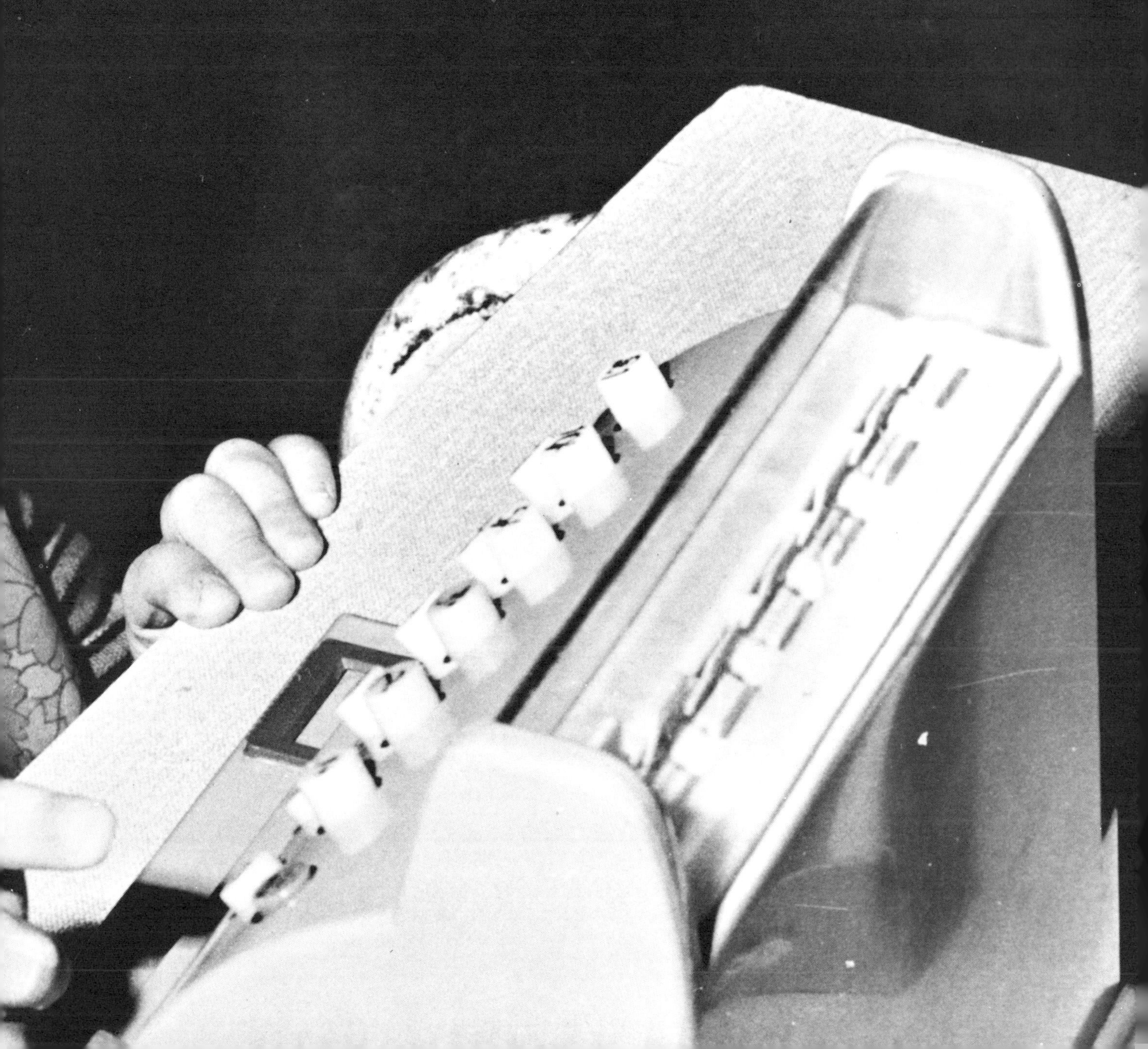

Michael Jackson

# PREPARING FOR PLAYGROUP Kate Moodie

## You

'BABY' IS ONE OF the first words. Children squeal it, struggling upright in their prams and pointing to a peer as if they'd spotted an angel. By the time your child is two, such behaviour may have convinced you that he needs more companions than just his mother, who in turn may find *Peek a boo* and *Round about the garden* are, like her, wearing a bit thin.

At this point many parents think that a playgroup would be the solution. Some don't know exactly what a playgroup is, but as Jill Archer has one and *The Observer* says they are okay, the surprised playgroup movement is finding itself with more applicants than it can take.

Most playgroups give preference to four year olds and then three year olds. They have learnt the hard way that although mothers are more than ready to register two year olds, the youngsters, however bright, just haven't the social or emotional development for a happy and productive experience. To turn a bunch of twos loose without their keepers at this age is to invite a bloodcurdling chorus of 'It's mine!' The most you can expect of your average two year old is pottering along near other children; he's months or even years away from 'Do you need some clay?' or 'Soon it will be my turn.'

What the under-three probably needs is a *Mother and Toddler Club*. Here the parent, gran or minder stays with the child throughout (usually) a weekly early-afternoon session. The little ones play with whatever is available; the mothers talk over the teacups or gather on rugs and cushions with the babies. As these are clubs, the parents are completely responsible for the children and the 'programme'. Some enjoy more than tea and chat, requesting toy exhibitions, demonstrations and lectures. In one London borough, an education department adviser links MTCs with further education. MTCs are not registered with Social Services, so you might have difficulty finding one. If word of mouth fails, Pre-school Playgroups Association (PPA) area organisers and advisers, health visitors and some vicars should know where to find them.

Many playgroups make their premises available to MTCs; if you use one you can assess whether its equipment is clean and whole, how warm, how noisy, how safe the premises are. If it is near your home, you may be tempted to put your child's name down for next year's playgroup, for there is much to be said for playing with neighbouring children.

## Shopping around for a playgroup

If the waiting list is discouragingly long or you aren't happy about, say, the acoustics or the outdoor space, you'll want to see what else is available. There are (but very unevenly distributed around the country) state nursery schools and classes, private nursery schools and prep schools, pre-school centres, day nurseries, child minders, home playgroups, and community playgroups.

Nothing in the law keeps some of these from calling themselves playgroups when really they are not, so your queries should be searching. Try your local Information Service, Citizens' Advice Bureau, or your health visitor. If you live in the wilds, write to County Hall, asking both Education and Social Services what's available in your area. If they don't reply adequately, write to the Pre-school Playgroups Association, asking for the nearest voluntary Area Organiser. (Don't expect replies without stamped addressed envelopes; postal charges are driving the most obliging charities into silence.)

In this article, I discuss only community playgroups held in public halls, but you should not overlook the *home playgroups*. Many are delightful and their scale is easier for a young child fresh from a secluded home. Some local authorities put all playgroups under 'child minders'; others just put home groups in that category.

The nice thing about most community playgroups is that, unlike schools, they let you watch the children at work.

People who say 'I'd be embarrassed to sing/work puppets/discipline a child in front of his parents' simply don't apply for super-

*Pages 28/29:* Bob Bray

From WHERE 114 (March 1976)

visor's jobs. You needn't expect to feel like a sore thumb; playgroups are used to being observed by pupils and students.

Unlike MTCs, where parents stay all the time, playgroups must be acceptable to Social Services departments; space, safety and personnel are therefore vetted before registration. But you'll also want to know about less static qualities, which are best assessed at first hand.

As supervisors are busy during playgroup sessions, and committee members are not always on the premises, it's advisable to write asking the playgroup for permission to observe a session or two. If you like, ask them to put down your child's name for next year. Pressing considerations about timing should be confided to print at the same time. It isn't usually thought wise (if you can avoid it) to couple playgroup entry with, say, a move from a familiar house or the arrival of a new baby. Most playgroups will try to include a new child in their permitted maximum before his name comes to the top of the list, if there are such special needs. Of course, if later your observations convince you the playgroup is not right for you, make some tactful excuse and remove his name.

Don't be deterred from the hunt for a playgroup by some behaviour problem or handicap. Most playgroups accept children with problems, from daytime wetting to epilepsy, and it's better to write about your problem than to hold whispered conversations over the child's head. Don't expect an immediate yes, however; the supervisor may first want to take advice, or to ask for extra voluntary help. There are *Opportunity Groups* for parents of very severely handicapped children; your doctor should know of these.

## Checklist for observing

Having made arrangements for someone else to take care of your child, present yourself at the playgroup and 'make like wallpaper'. Here's a brief checklist for an observing parent to use.

*First the adults*. Are there enough to read, to converse, to watch the swings, get the milk and label the paintings, store the collages and brief newcomers like yourself? The legal ratio is one to eight but some authorities say one to six and lucky playgroups have space for one to four. (There won't be classes that small again until sixth form or university; pure gold, unless the adults just chat among themselves. Playgroups are for that too, but after hours.) If the adults include grans and males and schoolkids, so much the better.

Do the adults give lots of directions or do they stay in the background, letting new activities arise out of the kids' imagination? Do they expect six-year-old behaviour from three year olds, like sitting through long dull stories? Are toilet accidents treated casually? Is discipline matter-of-fact and kindly, or do the adults resort to ridicule, exclusion or threats? If a child wants a cuddle, does he get it? Do the adults run an arts and crafts assembly line, making nine-tenths of the cotton wool bunnies or Squeezy lighthouses 'to take home to mummy'? Has the supervisor attended at least a year long playgroup course?

*What about the premises?* Most halls are architectural horrors, with too few ceilings and too little storage space; given that, has the committee done its best to make a happy place for children, creating a home corner for a small family's domestic dramas, a cosy cushioned book corner, a remote spot for noisy woodwork? If there is no playground, where is the nearest park and how often does the playgroup visit it? Are there enough big boxes, ladders, bricks and climbing toys, or is most of the equipment of the sort a child could get at home? Is there sand, paint, water, clay? Can people talk without raising their voices? Skip without slipping on paintings?

*Finally, playgroups are for parents* as well as kids. Does the playgroup take note that you too need friends and fun and information? Is someone trying to help you to make sense of the playgroup scene while you observe? Has a committee member called on you to make you welcome?

A good index to this aspect is the playgroup's notice board. It might show a map with the kids' houses ('Just one street away! We never knew!'); holiday postcards; an article from CONTACT, the PPA magazine; a 'phone number for a baby-minding club; a recipe for play dough or the words of an action song; the playgroup's constitution; notice of the next election for playgroup officers; explicit invitations to parents to attend evening meetings of the playgroup, the local branch of PPA, the further education or WEA playgroup courses. Is *You too can be a mother-helper* there to borrow? All, of course, in addition to the diary of rota-helpers, and where to contact committee members. People don't feel part of a group unless they are sure when and where they are welcome; without such communication a playgroup can be seen not as a co-operative venture but simply as a service, like the launderette.

At the opposite extreme, it can be a haven of help and goodwill, laughter and discovery. As a Glasgow mother said about her lonely, gloomy pre-playgroup days, 'See me? I used to be deid.' So it's worth looking for the right playgroup.

Of course, you won't find all the virtues anywhere. After all, community playgroups are run by parents, and some of them will have been on the scene just a few weeks longer than you, perhaps aware of the same inadequacies but not yet sure how to make things better. Even when a playgroup fails some of the suggested tests, if it still feels like a pretty good place to you, why not join? When your child enters playgroup, so do you. You can accept what can't be changed, and help improve what can.

## Your child

Having found a playgroup and been admitted at least to its waiting list, you'll want to start getting your child used to the idea. But not, I'd suggest, by announcing to him, or anyone except his father, that he's going to playgroup. I've seen a milkman, in a desperate search for a topic both intelligible to a child and smirkworthy to a parent, tell a three year old, 'Don't forget to take an apple and a slate!' Great-grandparents are apt to counsel a sprout to 'Do just what your teacher says, you hear?' The first produces confusion, the second immobility if taken literally, for a good playgroup 'teacher' directs as little as possible. Kids are also better without anxiety-provoking injunctions like 'Drink up your milk; you'll have to do when you get to playgroup, you know!'

## Are there helpful books?

There are lots now for parents. Look at the five-part series *Pre-school materials for parents* in WHERE 97 to 102. The PPA publishes useful books for parents including *Playgroup activities, Settling a child into playgroup, The playgroup movement* and *You too can be a mother-helper*. It is good that there is plenty for parents to read, for if you know what to expect, your child is likely to feel comfortable too.

All the picture books I've seen miss the mark. They use the word 'playschool' arousing expectations of meeting Gazonka or learning school skills. (Playgroups do a lot with pre-reading but are counselled not to teach the three Rs.) In its attempt to couple reassurance with a dramatic story line, *My brother Sean* creates worry . . . why is the little boy unhappy? *Cherry goes to playschool,* where the equipment picture would shame Disneyland; no playgroup could live up to such expectations. *Mr Longfoot,* like most of the above, offers interesting comparisons once a child knows about his own playgroup, but, like Cherry, the text is too long and his grotesque feet, which would amuse a five year old, might worry a three year old. A librarian friend says that a Topsy and Tim and a Ladybird book on going to school might be acceptable. Having visited the playgroup, you will get to know best which books might prepare and which confuse a child.

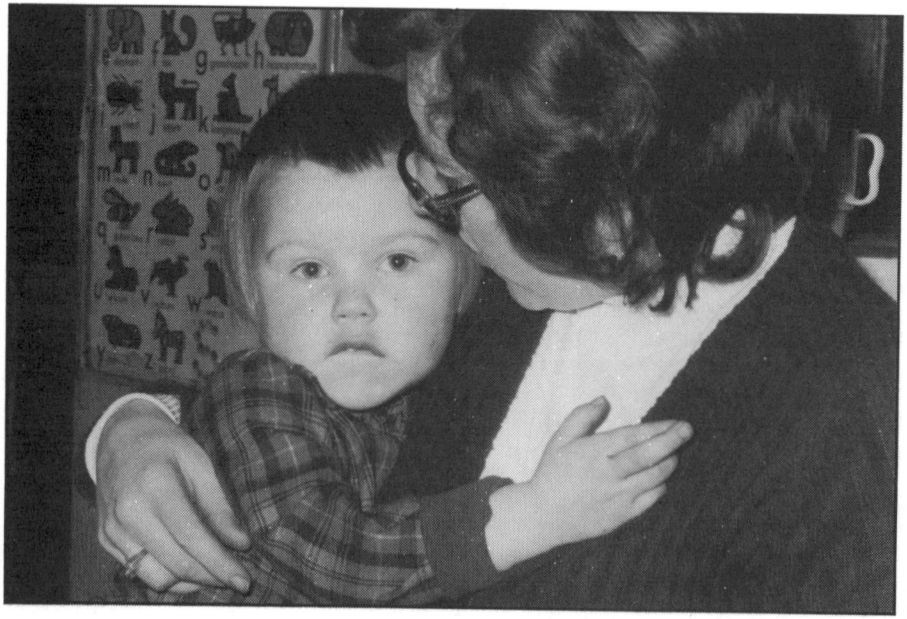

Bob Bray

## What does help?

Here are some positive suggestions which may help your child:

**1** – Ask the playgroup supervisor or secretary if any of the children live near your home. A child who sees familiar faces when he enters the playgroup is likely to feel elated.

**2** – Some children have dreadful hangups about getting mud, clay, paint or glue on their clothes; they refuse to finger-paint or model. You can help yours by providing such materials at home, and showing your unconcern 'as long as you are wearing playclothes'.

**3** – If you don't own them, invest in *70 action songs* (PPA), *This little puffin* (Puffin) and a good *Mother goose;* it's fun for kids to say things together at playgroup, and reassuring to know some rhymes already.

**4** – If you don't mind wasting a dozen straws per bottle, let your child experiment with drinking this way; it's a skill that's useful in many playgroups. (Most kids don't manage well until their fourth year, but it's fun trying.)

**5** – When the playgroup notifies you that there is a place for your child, arrange brief visits to start with after term begins. Most of the new children will have been absorbed by then, and the supervisor will have more time to make a good relationship with your child. *Don't make a fuss.* At the risk of sounding devious, I still wouldn't say 'Guess what! You're starting playgroup tomorrow!' The less excited he is, the better he'll sleep and the better he'll cope with the next day's experience. Just lay out his playclothes and say goodnight as usual.

Next day I'd take the child past the playgroup, ostensibly to a park or a shop, on foot if possible. Arrive perhaps 45 minutes late; you'll stay longer next time. Children may be playing outside, or there may be glimpses of interesting toys. If he asks to join the children (as he might in a public park) it's politic to warn, 'Very well, but we can't stay long'. If he doesn't ask, bring him inside while you give the supervisor something like feathers, or loo rolls or seedpods you've been saving for the children's play.

**6** – Your role now is to sit with some busy work on the sidelines while he begins to explore, sometimes alone, sometimes with a friendly child or the supervisor. It's important to stay where he left you; if he feels overwhelmed he'll need to see you, or to have a cling and a cuddle. The supervisor may put a low table and a few small playthings at your side; if other children are attracted by these, you and your child may be at the centre of a group. He'll find this an easier way of getting to know the children than playing away from you at this early stage.

**7** – If you stay all morning, remark on all the mothers and fathers coming to collect their children for dinner (or tea, if it is an afternoon session). Little children have no idea what 'Mum will be back in half an hour' means, but dinner is a recurring event; it may reassure him to remember this ritual when his mother eventually leaves him for a whole session.

**8** – But that time is not yet; you'll stay for at least a few more sessions, concealing, one hopes, your impatience about the other demands on your time. If he protests that he doesn't want to go to playgroup one day, give it a miss and go to the park instead; children do things more readily if they don't feel compelled. (Of course, playgroup budgets, being made up of parents' fees and the proceeds of jumble sales, don't allow for will-he-won't-he delays in payment; after your child is registered as a member of the playgroup, you'll be expected to follow the same payment procedure as the other parents.)

**9** – When you refer to tomorrow's plans, remember to say that 'we' not 'you, John' are going to the playgroup. The most independent child may balk if a solo flight is implied before he is ready. Soon he will notice that most of the playgroup parents help from time to time in various ways, but that at no time are they all there at once.

**10** – Make sure the children know where the lavatories are, and which they may use; this may be their first experience of a Gents and a Ladies!

**11** – Food is important. Try to come home to his favourite mid-day menu, prepared before you leave for playgroup. If he wants to, recall together some of the activities, stories or songs of the morning. Your enjoyment is part of his pleasure; the playgroup will be an extension of his home, and its interests will flow back and forth.

**12** – Ask the supervisor what name she likes the kids to use and avoid confusion by using it too when you talk about her. When one is only three, Mrs Smith, Auntie Bea, Beatrice and Beattie can sound like four different people.

## Possible problems

**1** – If, in spite of your keeping the entrance to playgroup casual, your child has been wildly enthusiastic about playgroup, quite happy about your leaving him, and euphoric in retrospect about the day's events, be prepared for a slight set-back in a few weeks; for some reason, such children often cool down a lot after a few sessions. It may have something to do with unreasonable expectations.

**2** – When you change your role from the mother who just happened to stop in with her child to being a regular parent-helper, your child may astonish you by clinging and/or cheeking, or even telling you to go home. It happens to most of us, bringing resentment and embarrassment to all but the most placid. All those weeks of preparation . . . for this? The supervisor will assure you that he's not like this at other sessions; salt in your wounds, maybe, but it's true. Attempt to keep him at the same distance as other children and he'll bring the house down. Playgroups usually regard the mother-helper's child as the child-of-honour for the day; he may pass the snacks, choose the story, sit on your lap or faff around on the periphery, elaborately casual.

**3** – If when you bring him some mornings he clings and bellows, listen carefully to his screams; some mean genuine distress, others are a bit staged. Stay if you think it best.

A neighbour with a car can usually get one through this stage, 'Mary's mum is collecting the children this morning.'

**4** – However satisfied a child is, he may at first be very tired by the variety, bustle and noise of his new life. If you find he is too weary to eat dinners, don't worry; bring some quick-energy nibbles to the playgroup when you collect him and try to forget all you've said about eating between meals. What you want is to boost his blood sugar so he can get home to a meal or a nap.

## Settling in

How long should you expect to devote to settling your child at playgroup? There's no answer, except as long as it takes. Some children require more tandem visits than others before they'll say 'You can go shopping now'. It could take months, or after three sessions you may both know that it's all right. The important rule is Never Sneak Off. Announce even brief absences: 'John, I'll be in the kitchen having coffee', 'John, I've run out of elastic for this clown suit, hold my scarf while I dash out to buy some more'. If he howls, take him with you, and try again when it seems opportune.

Your child must expect to see another mother in 'your' playgroup chair some day. The point at which yours becomes blasé may be the day a newer child enters playgroup.

If yours looks like being a long stay, consider the career of my friend Margaret, whose child seemed genuinely to need her presence for a whole year of settling in. In the process she became so interested that she turned into a mother-helper, a supervisor, a PPA area organiser and a playgroup tutor. She has since started two more playgroups.

If a playgroup doesn't seem quite right to you and your child, get together with some neighbours and start another; thousands of parents do it every year, and there are many areas where more are needed.

*Kate Moodie is editor of the PPA magazine,* CONTACT.

### where to find out more

The **Pre-school Playgroups Association** address is Alford House, Aveline Street, London SE11 5DJ; or for Scotland, 7 Royal Terrace, Glasgow G3 7NT.

Recent WHERE articles on playgroups include *Pre-school education: state provision and playgroups* (100); *Pre-school courses for parents* (104); *A rota for your playgroup* (105); *Re-cycling for pre-school mums* (106); and *Father's role in pre-schooling* (112). Back issues are available from ACE at 60p each.

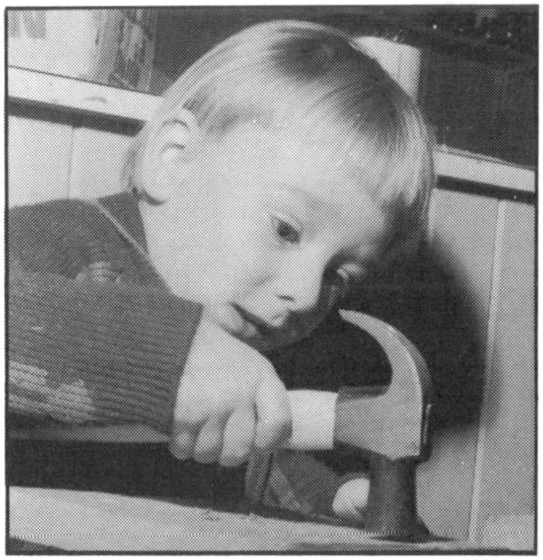

Bob Bray

# SETTING UP A NEIGHBOURHOOD NURSERY: a practical guide

When you want to find out how to do something, go to the people who have done it. This practical guide is based on the work of the Children's Community Centre in North London (see WHERE 98). The Centre is a neighbourhood-based nursery set up and controlled by parents. This guide is intended to provide useful information for those interested in setting up similar nurseries. Use it all, or select the advice which squares with your own circumstances and ideas.

## Money

It is helpful to draw up an estimate of your annual expenditure, including salaries, equipment and running costs. Work out the minimum you consider you need in order to keep going. Then work upwards from that figure. Money is available from various sources:

*Local council social services department* This is where the Children's Community Centre gets its money. Contact the Day Care department within Social Services. Try to find a sympathetic person to work through.

*Urban aid* Money is available for capital costs and running costs of 'suitable' projects. Seventy-five per cent of the money comes from the Home Office and 25 per cent from local government. You have to go through your social services department for support of your application. Ask them for advice on how to apply for urban aid money.

*Local education authority (LEA)* You might be able to get some money from your LEA but it will mean employing at least one trained teacher and probably being affiliated to the nearest nursery school. You are likely to lose some of your autonomy and control.

*Charities* You could apply to different charities for money (trust book listing the charities is available from public libraries). The politics of doing this is delicate as it lets the council off the hook – it is their responsibility to finance day care for the under-fives.

*Fund raising* As a last resort you could try to raise some of your own money (jumble sales, discos and so on). This is the worst method of obtaining money for at least two reasons: first it is another case of doing the council's work for it; and second it is a terrific drain on valuable time and energy.

## Premises

*Finding suitable premises* This is one of the most difficult tasks, particularly in inner London where there is so much pressure on all available property for housing people. A house is certainly preferable to a church hall.

First decide roughly where you'd like your centre to be and then look for empty houses, and houses about to be sold, in the area. You can discover who owns the houses by going along to the Rates and Valuation department of your local council and asking who the owners are. In this way you can discover which houses the council owns.

Next compile a list of empty council-owned houses which you think are suitable (include a garden if possible) and send it to the Housing department accompanied by a written proposal describing your project. Get support from the Day Care department if you can. Keep applying pressure until something happens.

Should all forms of 'peaceful' negotiation fail, some groups squat a house and ask questions later. Try to decide whether you would be content with a short-life house (like the Children's Community Centre) or whether to insist on something more permanent. Short-life houses are much easier to come by, but only put off the problem of accommodation rather than solve it.

*Insurance* Once you've got your house, and are ready to start, you must take out some insurance. Check if the local council has any insurance on the house. You will need to be insured for fire, theft, and damage to property and equipment, and you should also cover yourselves in case of accidents to children and workers. Check with your local citizens' advice bureau, or local law centre (if there is one), that you are adequately covered.

*Rates* You can apply to your council for rate relief on the grounds that you are providing a social service. The Children's Community Centre got a 100 per cent rate rebate on its house.

## Food

*Milk* You are entitled to provide free milk for the children in the nursery – a third of a pint per child per day. First obtain a milk registration form (WF/DNI5) authorized by your local authority. This confirms how much free milk your nursery is entitled to. Send it to: Department of Health and Social Security (DHSS), Room 7, AGD 6 Government Buildings, Honeypot Lane, Stanmore HA6 1AY, Middlesex (01-952 2311 Ext 255). DHSS sends a milk claim form to you. But you buy the milk first (from any dairy; get a receipt) and have to claim the money back from the DHSS (address as above) every three months.

*Bulk buying* Start a food co-operative among parents and workers and buy all your food in bulk from wholesalers. The food is cheaper and fresher, and the co-op is a good way to bring people together.

## Equipment

Contact your local council to see if it will supply you with the equipment provided in schools (you will have to pay, of course). In London the GLC supplies furniture, art



From WHERE 106 (July 1975)

materials and so on. For catalogues and requisition books for London apply to: Forms Officer, Southfields Depot, Kimber Road, London SW18. Some second-hand furniture (including tables, chairs, easels, water trays, bookshelves and so on) is occasionally obtainable from local education authorities. Write to your LEA to find out. In London the second-hand goods from schools are available from: Romford Supplies, 205 London Road, Romford, Essex (63673). Ring before you go to see what they have in stock. A lot of damaged material is now recycled back into schools because of the economic situation.

*Free or improvised materials* Get a large roll of white kitchen paper from your local printers. It is the end roll of newsprint. Get sheets of yellow drawing paper from the X-ray department of your nearest hospital. It is the backing paper from the X-ray film. Use large empty cardboard boxes for creative play (trains, boats, cars and so on). Tape around empty shoe boxes to close and reinforce them and use as building blocks. They're great for group-play as they're big. Save all empty cartons, packets and so on and use for 'junk-box modelling'.

*Compiled by Gill Pinkerton and the Children's Community Centre.*

## Where to find out more

For ideas about activities and improvised equipment:
*The playgroup book* by Winn and Porcher, Fontana, 40p (part 2 on activities).
*The Penguin book of playgroups* by Joyce Lucas and Vivienne McKennell, 80p (part 4 on playing and learning).
For reading on community child care:
*The day care book – the why, what and how of community day care* by Vicki Breitbart (Knopf, £2·30) available from Dillons, Malet Street, London WC1 (01–636 1577).
*The Children's Community Centre* pamphlet is available for 23p from 123 Dartmouth Park Hill, London N19.

# A ROTA FOR YOUR PLAYGROUP

## Eleanor Grey

MANY PLAYGROUPS have parents helping their regular, paid staff on a rota basis. This assistance is often necessary because local authority regulations require an appropriate adult/child ratio. It can also bring positive benefits to parents, children and staff.

There are arguments for and against a rota, and groups should work out what suits them best. But wherever a rota is used it needs to be carefully organised, and be seen by all concerned as fair.

It is not surprising that difficulties arise because, of course, some parents cannot help. They may be working or constrained by domestic circumstances: for example, a young baby who will need feeding. Some are prevented from coming on their allocated day by a last-minute emergency. Others forget. Another problem is that the number of sessions in a term is not usually divisible between all parents equally; some will inevitably be given more turns than others.

Parents' attitudes towards rota duty are, naturally, very mixed. Assisting in the play of a large group of under-fives is skilled and demanding work and not all mothers have a natural aptitude for it. Some thoroughly enjoy helping in a playgroup; others find the sounds of mass pre-school carpentry hard on the ears, and the whole business something of an ordeal. Even those who usually like helping may feel imposed upon if their willingness to take extra turns is taken for granted, or their other commitments and interests begin to suffer. It is only too easy for a group to drift into relying for essential assistance on a conscientious few.

Fruitful parent involvement must be based on providing opportunity and encouragement, not coercion. To make the provision of a playgroup place conditional on the parent's ability and willingness actively to participate cannot be justified, at least not as long as there is a scarcity of pre-school places. Parents must have the right to opt out of a rota. However, although parent-helpers are regarded as volunteers and are so when compared with paid playgroup staff, a rota for many playgroups is not an optional extra. So any opting out should not be at the inconvenience and expense of the rest. Economics do enter into it, because without a rota these groups would have to pay more staff and charge everyone higher fees. The parent who does not take part is being subsidised by the rest unless financial adjustments are made.

Some people disapprove of any financial element in a rota system: although non-financial forms of contribution may be sought which can be far less reasonable. For example, it has been suggested that working mothers who are not available for rota duty should be invited to wash and mend the playgroup's dressing-up clothes and overalls in their free time.

Nevertheless, many groups do use some kind of financial incentive. Some waive the fees for a parent-helper's child for the session at which she helps. Others fine mothers who miss their turn, although this can lead to anomalies.

A different scheme is used by a parent-run group in Southwark, south London. At the beginning of term all parents at St Faith's playgroup pay the treasurer a certain sum, over and above their fees. These contributions form a pool, out of which the parent-helper each day is given a fixed amount. The charge is worked out so that the total contributed by parents is expected to be equivalent, over the year, to the total handed out to parent-helpers. The charge is a kind of deposit.

The amount parents are charged is related to the number of mornings their child is down to attend and is calculated per child, so that those with two children at the playgroup pay double. But parents who are charged more are given more opportunities to take a turn on the rota and get their money back.

This scheme was discussed and accepted by a general meeting of the playgroup before it was introduced. We decided that the level of refund for each helper would be 50p a morning. This was an administratively convenient sum and compared logically with the staff's rates of pay. Other playgroups might want to make this sum more, or even less. But always remember that the larger the refund, the larger is the deposit required at the beginning of term, an important consideration where parents are financially hard-pressed. On the other hand in better-off areas a relatively high refund, such as £1 per session, could be appropriate.

At St Faith's playgroup it worked out that to permit a refund of 50p, the parents of a child who comes three times a week would need to pay 75p a term: those whose children come twice a week are charged 50p.

The parents like a system which is fair, and it has been running smoothly since it started, three years ago. Mothers or fathers

who help on an average number of occasions receive in refunds, over the course of time, the same amount that they pay in rota charges; they are financially neither better nor worse off. Those who cannot participate in the rota need not feel guilty, because they are making their contribution in the form of the rota charge. Since those who do help receive 50p on each occasion, a mother who does extra turns is compensated to a small degree for her time and effort. There is no difficulty now in finding someone to stay and help, even at very short notice.

Several children at St Faith's have their fees paid by the local authority and careful thought was given to whether parents in straitened circumstances should be asked to contribute the rota charge. For various reasons it was decided to treat everyone alike as a general rule, but it is within the treasurer's discretion to make special arrangements.

Once the initial calculations have been done, this refund scheme is simple to operate. Different charges would of course be needed in different playgroups, according to how they are organised, but any group could work it out for themselves. If more than one set of children is catered for, the calculation is done separately for each set.

**The formula**

This is the formula to follow:

1 – decide what the parent-helpers should be paid

2 – then for each child *multiply* that by the number of parent-helpers on duty each session

3 – then by the number of sessions the child is down to attend each week

4 – then by the number of weeks in the playgroup year

5 – *divide* the resulting figure by the number of children on the register for those sessions.

6 – then *divide* by 3 to get the amount to be paid each term.

That gives you the charge for each term. So if the payment settled on is £1; there are two helpers each session; the mother sends her child for three mornings a week; the year lasts 37 weeks; and the group has 40 children on the register, the calculation is:

$$\frac{£1 \times 2 \times 3 \times 37}{40 \times 3} = £1{\cdot}85$$

You can do the calculation afresh for each term, taking into account the different number of weeks in each term. But we have found it better to work out the deposit in the way described (*ie* by calculating for the whole year and dividing by 3) rather than doing new sums each term.

*Eleanor Grey is on the committee of the National Campaign for Nursery Education.*

# COUNTRY CHILDREN Carla Phillips

**Living in the country is not the pastoral paradise many people imagine it to be. For the under-fives it can be particularly damaging. The problem? Isolation. We report on what happened when a playgroup was started up in one Norfolk village.**

EVERYTHING ORGANISED in the countryside is done by 'outsiders'. Our playgroup was no exception. Country life has certain well advertised advantages: clean air and lots of open space, more cows and corn than cars and concrete. But the disadvantages, such as isolation and loneliness, are rarely as well publicised.

People who live in rural areas are often quite unable to benefit from all that open space. If their house has a tiny garden, or if they are tenants on a farm where every inch of land is given over to agriculture, there may be little or no play space for their small children. Outside the villages, people are scattered widely about the countryside, often with no neighbours, and no regular means of getting into the nearest village.

## Beginnings

It was nearly eight years ago that I first tried to start a playgroup in my Norfolk village. I put a few signs up in the papershop window, but had little response beyond a few tart suggestions that I set up as a childminder, while the local mothers worked at the vegetable scraping plant. This response wasn't entirely surprising; country people are often deeply suspicious of any innovation, sensing – probably rightly – that anything new will only drive an additional wedge between the generations.

My second attempt to start a playgroup, six years later, was more successful. Many people from 'away' had moved into our area. There was an overwhelming amount of publicity in the newspapers and on radio and television about pre-school education. And this time I was not alone in my attempt, for there were now two prime movers – a Glaswegian and myself (from New York City).

We started by spying out possible sites for the playgroup. The village hall, built on the village outskirts, was one possibility. Better still, the local primary school, built in the '50's as one of the last five to 14 all-in schools, had a few empty classrooms.

We approached the headmaster. He was not difficult to persuade. He was very aware of the problems of certain of the children in our area, who attend school for the first time at the age of five. Some of these children are completely unaccustomed to the sight of other children. Many have severely limited vocabularies; they come from illiterate homes; occasionally children are not even accustomed to using a knife and fork. Anything that might attempt to reach these children and improve their lot was desirable.

The headmaster offered us a classroom to meet in to organise things, if sufficient people in the area were interested. So, we put up posters in all the villages within a three-mile radius of the school, stating that a meeting to form a playgroup was going to take place, naming time and place. That first meeting attracted over 20 women, and from amongst them we formed a committee, scheduled fund-raising events in all the villages to be served by the playgroup, named a tentative date for the start of the playgroup, and planned another general meeting with suitable officials from the social services.

## Coming in

By that next meeting, we were really on the move. We quickly amassed tricycles, doll's prams, some books and puzzles, and raised enough money for the raw materials for a climbing frame and wendy house to be made by a handy-dandy dad. We appointed our leaders for the three mornings a week, and a rota for supplementary helpers. We designed a chart for the mothers' rota, leaving the individual mothers to fill in the blank spaces when and where they chose.

Of course, many of the children who attended from the first were the children of 'outsiders' or 'intruders'. But many were the children of the *bona fida* natives, due, no doubt, to all the propaganda in the media. There were only about 16 children attending at first, though we had room for 24. Then one day, one of the fathers, canvassing for votes at local election time, mentioned to the play leaders that he had come across a woman with small children – just the type that could use a playgroup. Would we go and visit?

Miles from anywhere, almost into another century, in a farm worker's cottage (two up,

From WHERE 103 (April 1975)

two down and running damp), we found a couple with three small children. The eldest, a boy of five, was taken to school by minibus. His three-year-old sister rarely saw a living soul outside her own family. The mother, affected perhaps by living in such isolation, had developed agoraphobia some years previously. She had recovered somewhat, but was still barely sociable. She seemed interested in the playgroup as her little girl was very lively, and obviously needed something. But she explained that as her husband only earned the farm worker's basic wage, our fees of 40p a week, plus the cost of petrol for a six-mile round trip journey, three times a week, made it out of the question. And even if we could get the little girl down to the school on the morning minibus, her husband's half-hour dinner break simply wasn't long enough to fetch the child back home.

We invited the mother, her small girl and tiny baby, down to the playgroup one morning when we were able to arrange for her return journey – just to see if they liked it. The little girl played happily all morning, and her mother was delighted. She became determined to make playgroup a regular occurrence for her child. But we all found that after asking everyone in sight to provide transport – in vain – the only other possibility left was the social services. After a great deal of persuasion, they agreed to pay for the taxi home for this little girl, and this service was also taken advantage of by another child from an equally remote family living in another cottage on the same estate.

Because the social services had been helpful about providing transport for these children, we were kindly disposed towards them when they approached us, and asked if we would accept a mongol boy into the playgroup. While we felt that as a general policy we would have to be careful of preserving the equilibrium of the group, in order not to end up as a 'dump' for problem children, we accepted the little boy immediately. It worked beautifully; it was very difficult to detect that he was a mongol in the first place – and he was also blessed with a mother whose wild sense of humour made her invaluable as a playgroup helper.

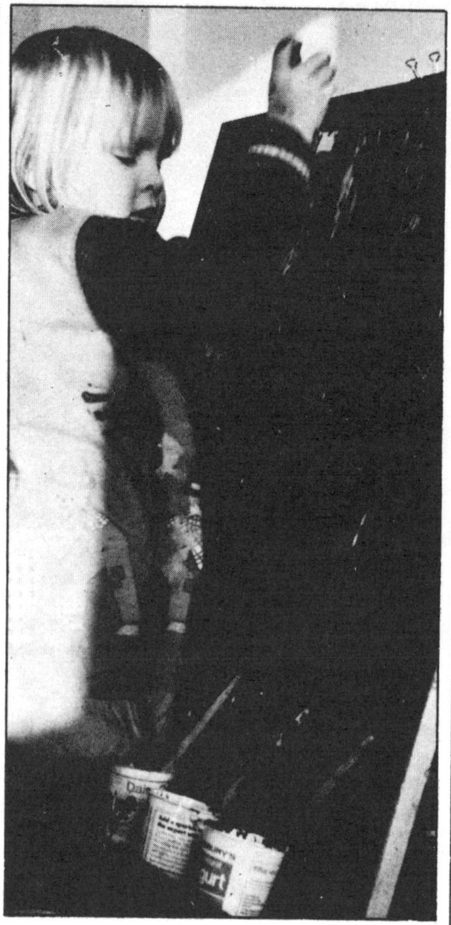

Bernard Phillips

## Harvest

For most of the country parents, the most visible advantage of a playgroup, outside of companionship, lies in the facilities and equipment it offers. Most of our parents couldn't begin to afford a climbing frame or a wooden wendy house, or some of the sophisticated and beautifully designed toys we have gathered together. But most of the parents have enlarged their horizons by seeing their children playing with things *they* never thought of using – such as water, pastry, or musical instruments made out of everyday objects. A few mothers confessed that it gave them something to actually talk about with their children for the very first time.

We deliberately tried to keep the playgroup informal in organisation; we don't have formal periods of everyone doing the same thing except at milk time, which we combine with a sing-song. Sometimes the intoxicating atmosphere – half club, half mad tea-party – stimulates the mothers present and a good time is had by all. But there are other times when it is sickening to see mothers destroying their children's paintings before their eyes.

Even though most of the parents earn very low incomes, their children turn up carefully and exquisitely dressed. There is the occasional really scruffy child – stinking of pee and reeking of perfume – but most children arrive looking impeccable. And they are expected to keep themselves tidy and clean at all costs. For some of the mothers, one can appreciate their problems; washing is a real hassle in a house with one cold tap in the kitchen. For these children, any freedom to mess about (with an apron on), any apparent chaos, is quite new. No wonder they had seemed bewildered during their first months of school.

The playgroup moves onto the school playing fields whenever weather permits. The climbing frame, barrels, wendy house, triangles, wheels, buckets and spades – all are moved by the mothers and children. During the school recess, the older children usually wander over to the little ones: a thrill for all. Our playing fields overlook a marsh where cows graze, a field used for wheat or sugar beet, and a cottage garden where chickens are kept – this is quite a bonus.

## Norfolk untamed?

After our first year, the school's headmaster pronounced himself delighted with the 'results'. At the very least, several miniature Attila the Huns and Genghis Khans have been 'tamed'. School-parent relations have improved. But, alas, this is not a perfect world, and several problems remain.

For a start, many country people still cannot take advantage of playgroups. While Norfolk social services is full of good wishes and sweet smiles, it seems unwilling to give concrete help by providing transport for children from remote places, unless family

## Where to get more information

Very little research has been done and little advice is available on the problems of young children in isolated rural areas. A minority of children are affected so no funds are provided for research and little practical help is given.

WHERE 29 featured an article *Are country children behind town children?* based on research done by Frank Barr on urban and rural differences in ability and attainment *(Educational research* February 1958). We have been unable to trace any relevant research or practical advice later than that!

The Scottish Pre-school Playgroups Association, Playgroup House, 7 Royal Terrace, Glasgow G3 7NT can give some advice for the under-fives. Brenda Crowe's book *The playgroup movement* (Allen and Unwin, £2·75) contains a section on playgroups in different types of community, including rural areas.

General books on pre-schooling include:

*The Penguin book of playgroups* by Lucas and McKennell (Penguin 80p)

*The pre-school years* by Willem van der Eyken (Penguin education, 65p).

*Two to five* a handbook for students and teachers by Marianne Parry and Hilda Archer (Macmillan, £1·55)

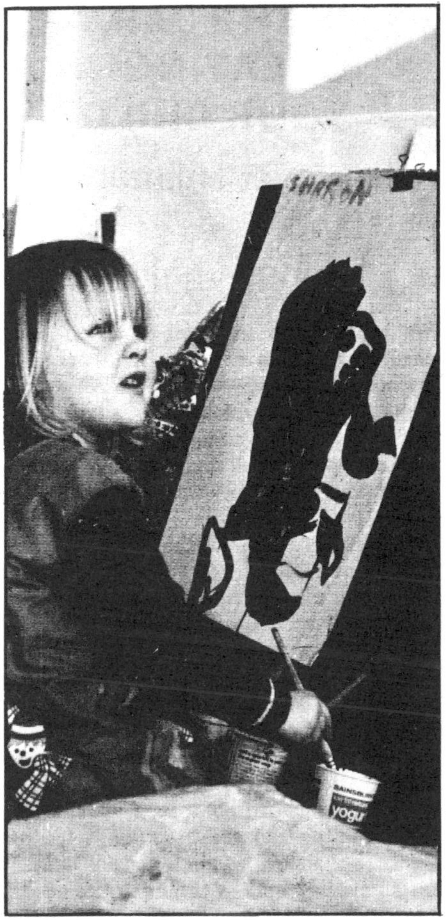

Bernard Phillips

problems are so dire that a social worker must be directly involved. I feel that this puts playgroup organisers and leaders into a delicate position; in order to get a child who will clearly benefit from it into the playgroup, the parents must be persuaded by the playgroup to call in the social services. This could lead to very unpleasant meddling.

Ordinary families, living on low incomes, who don't want the SS butting into their affairs, simply won't take the advantages available, no matter how much they'd like their children to attend playgroup. Sadly, many of these mothers are very willing to pay playgroup fees ('It's better than sweets, isn't it!'), and desperately want their children to go – it's the costs of transport that they can't rise to.

There is another problem for these people in inaccessible places – what happens when their children reach the age of four. Then they are entitled to attend school mornings, if their parents can fetch them at lunchtime. So once again, those children whose parents have cars or who live near enough to the school benefit. Norfolk seems unwilling to foot the transport bill unless the need is dire, dreadful, absolute and exceptional. It should not be so.

We have had a lot of encouragement and pleasant visits from the LEA and the social services, but have had very little direct help from any official body whatever. Transport remains our first priority, but we would dearly love to pay the leaders a really economic wage – perhaps linking it to the completion of a further education course. But we see little chance of any aid to playgroups from our LEA.

Lately, our playgroup's popularity has caught up with us. We have had to open for another morning – and we are fully booked each session. We now use the school hall one morning a week, with all the school's PE apparatus set up – a real monkey party. This great demand has meant that we've done little scouting around the outlying farms and hamlets to see if there are any more children that really need us. But it doesn't mean that they're not there.

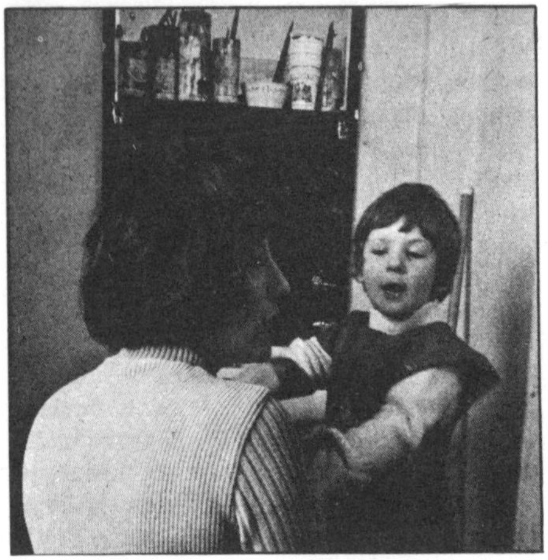
John Rocha

# PRE-SCHOOL COURSES FOR PARENTS

## Shirley Toulson

**Parents want courses to help them understand the development and fulfil the needs of pre-school children. It's really the logical step on from the proliferation of books and kits aimed straight at mums and dads with young children. But it is a demand that cannot yet be fully satisfied. So now is a good time to discuss just what courses are available, what they will tell you and how to choose the right course for your particular needs.**

I'VE FOUND FOUR REASONS why parents want these courses:

1 – they want to know more about their own child and so become a more effective and understanding parent;

2 – they are involved in a playgroup and want to add to their skill and ability in arranging the most useful experiences for both the children and the mother-helpers;

3 – they feel that, even though their own children have reached school age, they would like to continue working with the under-fives;

4 – they wish to embark on a course that will enable them, in their turn, to become tutors to new generations of mothers and playgroup supervisors.

If you fall into that third category you may find you are lucky enough to live in an area which provides a 'counselling' course to help you decide which type of work with young children you would now like to turn to.

The three types of courses – for mothers, supervisors and tutors – form a pyramid. With more people wanting the first type of course than the other two, there are more opportunities for going on a supervisors or tutors course. Many people, who like Mrs Maureen Huntley from Southampton, are professionally concerned with pre-school playgroup courses, would prefer to turn the pyramid upside down when considering their value. They feel that the courses for mothers are by far the most important part of the work.

These mothers' courses are usually quite informal. They often take place as part of the mother and toddler clubs that are now springing up throughout the country. On such a course mothers learn about the importance of play in all aspects of a young child's development. Later they learn the best ways of settling a child in playgroup and of gradually weaning him from the very close early bonds with one adult.

The courses for playgroup supervisors and mother-helpers run for a somewhat longer period. For the most part they are run as part of the LEA further education service, and usually take place on one day a week over three 10-week terms. Similar courses are also run on an evening basis, and some are organised by the Workers' Educational Association (WEA) or by university extra-mural departments rather than by the local education authority.

*Fees* No two areas are exactly alike nor is it at all possible to be specific about fees. To give one example, students in Doncaster pay £2·65 for a two-term course at either the college of technology or at the further education centre. Some authorities charge much more, while others are able to subsidise the course so heavily that fees are virtually waived. In some areas it is the custom for individual students to pay their own fees, in others these are assumed to be the responsibility of the playgroup to which the student is attached. So check at your local FE college or phone your local education office to see how your area works.

*Numbers* The numbers of students on the courses also vary considerably from place to place. Most tutors are loath to take on more than 30 students, because so much practical work is involved. In fact tutors usually confess that a group of 15 students is nearer the ideal number. Yet if people with pre-school children want to go on a playgroup course, they want to do it while the children are under-five. They can't afford to wait until next year. So the tutors don't like running a waiting list either.

*Qualifications* It's important for students to realise that these courses are an end in themselves. In some areas you may be given a certificate of attendance if you get to more than 75 per cent of the sessions. But the tutors and the people concerned with organising the courses are strong in their resistance to pressure from some quarters that a form of certificate should be awarded.

The Pre-School Playgroups Association (PPA) is equally concerned that the playgroup supervisors' courses should not be tied to any sort of paper qualifications. In the first place they fear that some of the people who have the most to offer the playgroups would be frightened of taking a course that they thought would put them to a pass/fail test; and in the second both the PPA and the further education departments consider that there is little point in awarding certificates which mean nothing as professional or employment qualifications. As one mother said, 'my own child's birth certificate is the best bit of paper I can show for this job'.

**What goes on**

To get the most out of your playgroup supervisor's course you should naturally be attached to a playgroup, and prepared to undertake a lot of practical work during the course. The tutors in charge of these courses will visit their students in their playgroups as



From WHERE 104 (May 1975)

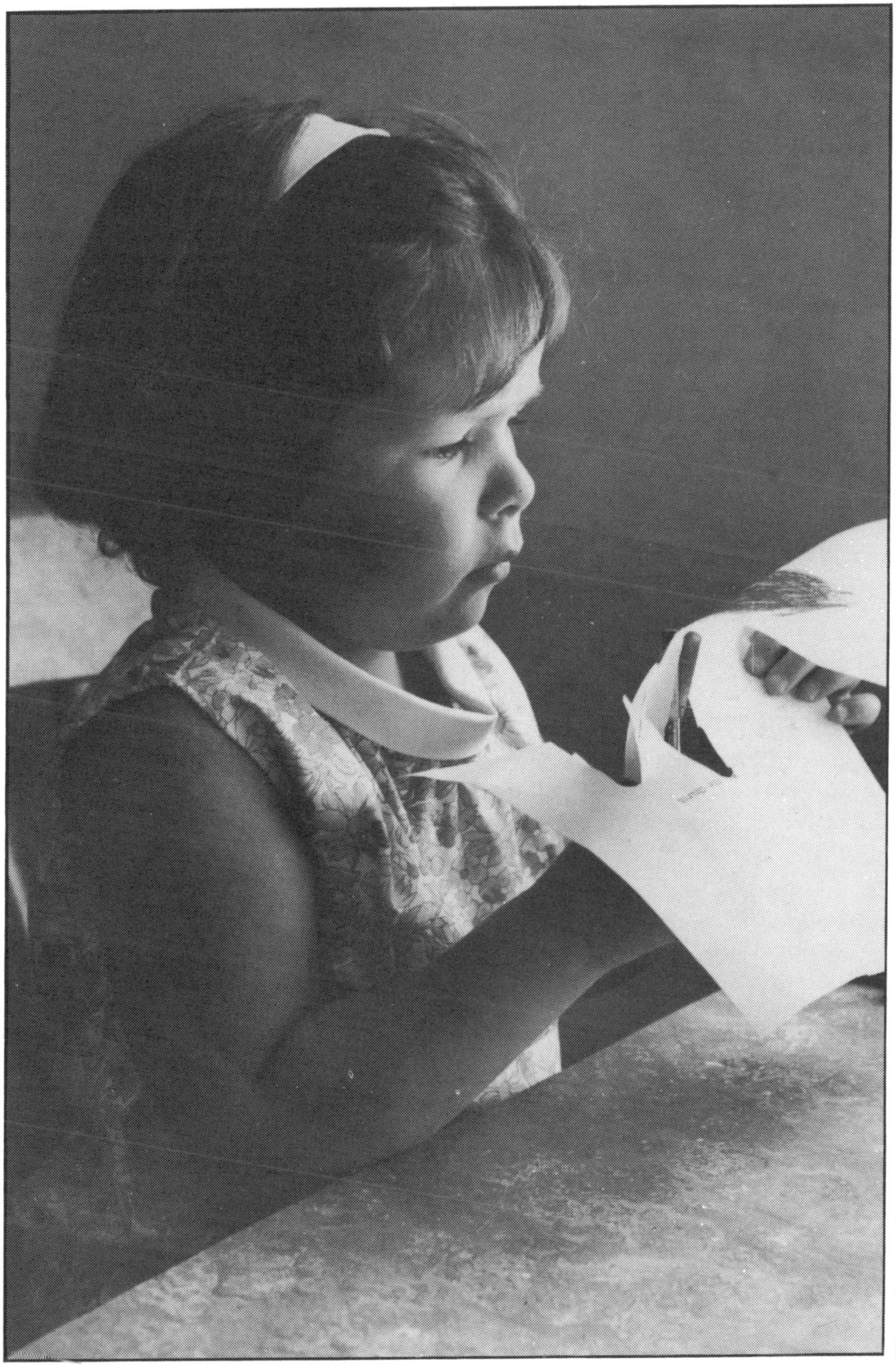

Dona Haycraft

often as possible, though for reasons of distance and time this isn't always easy. There is a great shortage of good tutors; their time is precious and travelling is costly in both hours and money.

Although the greatest emphasis is laid on the practical aspects of the course, many tutors hope that the students will be prepared to do some reading and occasional written work. In the best courses the reading will go beyond the textbooks on playgroup management, the many excellent guides on practical activities with young children, and the studies of early childhood development. Students will be encouraged to explore the imaginative literature of childhood, such as Laurie Lee's *Cider with Rose* (Penguin, 60p).

All the tutors stress that what they are offering is not a modified version of the training given either to nursery teachers or to nursery nurses. A playgroup makes completely different demands from either the nursery class or the day nursery, and the people who work in one need different skills. For this reason, the best courses are set up after full consultation with the training officers of the Pre-school Playgroups Association.

**Establishing a pattern**

In July 1974 the PPA held its own training conference at Leicester university. It was then that the general pattern of the courses, which I have outlined, was agreed on in principle. One of the most important recommendations to come from that conference stated that 'the PPA should continue to work with the Department of Education and Science and the Department of Health and Social Security towards playgroup and other related training', and that the people involved in discussions about these courses should look forward to other forms of training in the community development fields.

Mrs Huntley estimates that about one-third of the students who have taken her one-year supervisors' course, go on to take a further course which leads to other forms of work with young children, or to becoming tutors themselves. But she warns, 'You can't train tutors, you can only grow them.'

However there is now a move towards putting the Pre-School Playgroup tutors' course into line with the Further Education Teachers' certificate awarded by the City and Guilds of London institute. Yet as Joan Fazackerley, chairman of the PPA training committee, is at pains to stress, these courses and especially the supervisors', are not run for young paperchasers'.

The PPA has always acknowledged that what happens at home is the most important part of a young child's development, and so all the courses are primarily designed to help and support mothers and the people who work with them. Mrs Huntley is sure that in order to tutor such a course a person must have an enormous humility and a real respect for the astounding job that most mothers do, frequently in very difficult circumstances.

**How to choose**

You are the only person who can decide which type of course is best suited to your present needs. You certainly don't have to be an active member or even belong to the PPA in order to go on a course, but certainly someone from your local PPA would be the best person to advise you if you have any doubt as to whether it would be most valuable for you to go on a mother's or a supervisor's course; or whether having taken a supervisor's course you could gain from repeating that experience before you go on to any other form of training. And if you are in the fortunate position of being able to choose between two or three different courses in your area, the PPA people can probably help you decide which one will suit you best.

It cannot be emphasised too strongly how much any course concerned with pre-school children depends on personal relationships. Very often a course will build up round a particular tutor whose work is well-known in the area. If that is the case in the place where you live, you will find that the best way to find out about the best courses is by chatting with other mothers.

Before you embark on a supervisor's course, you must satisfy yourself that you can reasonably expect to meet its demands. These are basically that you will be able to put in a fairly regular attendance; and that you are prepared to give up some time to working in a playgroup if you are not doing so already. Don't embark on it if you want paper qualifications, or if you are looking for hints on how to teach your own or anyone else's baby to read.

These courses have something far more valuable to offer. They can give you an awareness of the needs of young children, and show you how these needs can be met both at home and in the community. People often complain, with some justification, that mothering is an isolated business. It needn't be. One of the best possible reasons for choosing to go on a course concerned with pre-school children is that it will put you into contact with other parents, who are doing something positive to ensure that they really enjoy their children's early years.

*Shirley Toulson was until recently the editor of 'Child education'.*

*Here is an example of the pre-school courses being run in one area of England:*

**Living and working with young children**: short courses for parents of young children and playgroup helpers.

These courses are planned to be used flexibly in a variety of ways. They can be taken singly or one after the other. They will be held according to demand and if there are enough people in one area a course can be held locally.

**Living with young children** (fee 75p) A course planned to help give parents and people working in playgroups more understanding of the early years of a child's life. Six weekly two-hour sessions.

**Playgroup activities: 1** (fee 75p) This is intended to help those who want to start a playgroup and have no previous experience. It will discuss how best to provide for the basic activities and how to make the best use of premises and equipment. Six weekly two-hour sessions.

**Playgroup activities: 2** (fee 75p) In this course the playgroup activities will be explored more fully with reference to the young child's development and the adult's role in the playgroup. Six weekly two-hour sessions.

**The playgroup course** (fee £7.50) This course is intended for those who already have some experience of working with young children and who wish to take more responsibility in a playgroup. Students should be attached to a playgroup or prepared to become attached to one for the purpose of studying. They will be asked to do some observation and preparation in their own time. One day a week for one year.

**Theories of child development**: a comparison of some theories of child development. (Fee 75p). Supplementary course for those who have completed the playgroup course and wish to study further. Six weekly two-hour sessions.

Bob Bray

# 4 Getting it together

# Getting it together

**We present a guide to the books, kits, toys and other materials which parents of pre-school children are most likely to find useful at home. It has been compiled by a panel of three pre-school experts—Brenda Crowe, national adviser to the Pre-school Playgroups Association; Mollie Clarke, senior adviser for nursery and infant education to Devon county council; and for part four, Joanna Matthews of the Parents Postal Bookshop in Cumbria.**

## 1: BOOKS ON EARLY LEARNING THEORY

**How to raise a brighter child** by Joan Beck (Souvenir £2.25, Fontana 60p)

*Brenda Crowe* When Joan Beck writes about bringing up babies from birth to 18 months she achieves a happy balance between the needs and abilities of the baby, and the needs and abilities of the parents to respond. For much of the time this balance is in evidence at the next stage, three to six years – but here the pressure element comes through strongly. No matter how many times a sensitive person reiterates: 'Don't teach formally . . . make a game of it . . . stop the minute the activity is no longer giving pleasure', it cannot possibly be assumed that parents are all able to respond with this degree of sensitivity – and it is so much easier to do harm than good when the parent/child relationship becomes the teacher/child relationship.

By pressure I mean this: is it really true that 'a bus trip is much more meaningful to a small child if you help him fit it into an overall concept about transportation'? I well remember needing the weekly bus ride to market as a silent oasis for *me*; and I also remember watching the children watching on those trips. Almost always they were silent, sometimes dreamy-silent lulled into a world of their own by the jogging of the bus; sometimes alert-silent, with eyes darting, heads turning, or even jumping up and turning round for a longer glimpse at something arresting. It was always fascinating to pick up snippets of observation casually mentioned days later, and to note how the children tended to notice quite different things.

What should we make too of 'Many of your happiest hours with your child will be times when you share his adventurous thinking and work together on creative products'? I know it says 'you share *his* adventurous thinking', but our experience with literally thousands of mothers in playgroups and on playgroup courses suggests that many will read those words and translate them as 'I will help him by guiding his thinking with my own'.

What about the recipe for flour and salt dough mixed with water to the 'right' consistency? A creative child will also need to experiment with the 'wrong' consistency. It is precisely this morality of 'right' and 'wrong' that parents should not accept unthinkingly but be exploring for themselves.

If books about bringing up children are to help parents too, they need to play down the 'teaching' and actively encourage the listening and watching. This book almost does it, but not quite.

*Mollie Clarke* The book is described as a first-rate guide to the methods by which a child can be taught, in his own personal style and at the correct speed during the important early years. It is also an attempt to translate in language which parents will understand, the findings of research on early learning and the cognitive development of pre-school children.

The first chapters attempt to trace a link between early stimulus on the part of parents and 'success' in later school life. Joan Beck blames play-orientated attitudes for failed potential later on. Three chapters are concerned with practical ways of effecting early stimulation of cognitive awareness – early or accelerated learning from birth to six. The message that pram and playpen-bound babies are cut off from vital areas of essential learning may reconcile parents to the prospect of unleashed crawlers making sensory experiments with a rich variety of materials over a wide area of house and garden.

I would question the author's belief that play and work are mutually exclusive. She feels work attitudes and curricular beginnings are not developed from play interests, but that specially devised materials and activities be used. For an opposite view look at the Schools' Council pre-school project (*Pre-school education* by Marianne Parry and Hilda Archer, Macmillan £3.95) which demonstrates the structuring of play which nursery teachers and good playgroup leaders now take in their stride.

Although this book may reflect the hopes of some parents, it describes conditions and priorities in a minority of present-day schools. In sensible expert hands all will be well. But practised by less skilled and more anxious parents, the kind of acceleration recommended could go wrong. And if it goes wrong it may produce anxiety and neurosis and the exact opposite of the desired effect.

**Reading and writing before school** by Felicity Hughes (Cape £2.25)

*Brenda Crowe* This is a deeply disturbing book because the writer's enthusiasm for Dr Glenn Doman (*Teach your baby to read* Cape £1.95), and for her own application of his methods to her two small daughters, could easily tempt parents to follow her example. It all sounds so easy, and such fun, to those who don't know much about



From WHERE 97 (October 1974)

children, or who don't ask themselves deeper questions.

Do we really want to expose our two year olds to systematic teaching of *anything* five times a day? It is significant that sometimes Felicity Hughes dropped the lessons for a few days if she sensed pressure. But she reports that when she asked them if they were ready to resume, they agreed – did she never wait to see if they would ask first? Just how dominant has this teaching made the mother in the mother/child relationship? Has this constant emphasis on looking at, and understanding, written symbols added to, or detracted from, the children's ability to look and wonder at animals, flowers and objects? The mother says, as her final word, that 'a tiny child has the right to enter these worlds, if for no other reason than that he, like me, gains enormous pleasure just from seeing the patterns in things' – she seems to be concentrating on sight to the exclusion of feeling.

The only mention of the father is: 'He helped by asking to be shown the blackboard when he came home: he was led importantly to the children's room and given a reading lesson'. There is no hint of family life, no mention of any other form of unobtrusive, loving training; no mention of the children's play; no mention of playmates, or of conversations overheard and possibly indicating whether or not the children lost or gained overall by this early addiction to books.

To be fair, it looks as though her methods might be helpful in the teaching of deaf children or non-English-speaking children. where there is an urgent need to back up physical and visual communication – if sounds are impossible, or very difficult, then it might be easier to establish deeper communication through the use of large symbols.

But ordinary loving, well-balanced parents will, I'm sure, want a much less obsessive approach to reading: and those who are tempted to try this method are likely to find that family relationships come under such strain that their children have missed out all along the line.

*Mollie Clarke* Felicity Hughes bases her innovatory ideas on a somewhat simple premise *ie* that just as children learn to hear sounds, they should also – and at the same time – learn to *see* them. Daughter Gwynneth at two years two months has read two story books and has a vocabulary (sight) of 70 words. She then graduates to two alphabet books. At the end of the third month she knows, without hesitation, all the sounds. After this comes combinations involving use of colour. At the end of the fourth month she can translate, again without hesitation, a large number of combinations.

This is how Gwynneth reads the word 'proud':
Mother covers all letters but p.

*Gwynneth* p
Mother uncovers pr
*Gwynneth* pr
Covers all but ou
*Gwynneth* Oh yes, ou
Shows prou
*Gwynneth* proud
*Mother* (*excited*) Very good – now what's this little letter (d)?
*Gwynneth* du
*Mother* That's right – so now the word says prou . .
*Gwynneth* proud
*Mother* Oh clever (*hugs and exclamations*)
*Gwynneth* What does proud mean mummy!

Chapter five is a dangerous one. It attempts to answer the question 'How much time will it take?' by giving a detailed, but approximate, programme similar to that followed by her own two children. There are obvious dangers here for mothers without Mrs Hughes's education, experience and enthusiasm as there are for children without Gwynneth's ability and drive. There is also a divergence between the view of infant and primary education apparently held by the author and current practice.

Some parents may have difficulty in assimilating the rather detailed but unrelated ideas: others may think they are able to arrange better programmes for their own children.

---

**Learning and playing** by Eileen Elias (Pitman £1·80)

---

*Brenda Crowe* This is a valuable bird's-eye view of the wider field of early education. It is not a detailed account of what parents can do at home in the first two or three years, but it does make the point that the really important job for the parents is to 'get through' to the child as a person. Language is set in the context of communication between parents and child, and the emphasis is on *listening* to the child, and responding with encouragement rather than 'teaching'. Advice is sound and wise.

There are clear explanations of what is meant by the terms nursery school, private nurseries, playgroups, infant schools, formal and progressive schools, independent schools. The book also gives helpful explanations of the mysteries of the integrated day, team teaching, streaming, audio-visual aids, sex education, the new maths, ITA, environmental studies, and a sensitive section on children with special needs *eg* mentally handicapped, maladjusted, physically handicapped, autistic and gifted.

There is plenty of advice once a child is near to entering school as to what to do, who to see, what to explain, what to ask for, if your child isn't happy at school – or if you aren't happy about what goes on. The difficulties of both teachers and parents are outlined, and there is strong positive encouragement to establish a good parent/school relationship.

*Mollie Clarke* This book sets out to explain how a young child's needs can be met in a variety of ways and by many different people in the family, playgroups, nursery classes and primary schools. Its main source is clearly the Plowden report.

Eileen Elias stresses the importance of communication between parent and child and the quotation from Dr Spock about early reading is reassuring if not fashionable. 'Often the parents themselves are more ambitious than they realise . . . the child senses their delight and responds with greater interest.' The suggestion that parents should have pre-school consultations with their future teachers is good. Child guidance treatment, on the other hand, is made to sound as easily available as influenza injections and the question of expert diagnosis and the pressing problem of waiting lists have been avoided.

There is advice on how to start playgroups, how to provide children with social experiences outside playgroups, how to select an infant/primary school and how to prepare the child for entry plus useful suggestions and ways in which to pursue these topics at greater depth. The book also explains current educational jargon.

---

**How to help a child at home** by Michael Newby and Kathleen Hartley (Home and School Council available from 17 Jacksons Lane, Billericay, Essex. 25p)

---

*Brenda Crowe* This is a concise and helpful working paper, offering advice and explanations cheerfully and sensibly. There are also valuable lists of books to read aloud, books for older children, music for listening, addresses of toy and equipment firms, lists of hobbies, and a list of addresses of national associations.

In short, a good guide in itself, and pointing the way forward for those who want to extend their reading and questioning.

*Mollie Clarke* This slim booklet assumes that parents and teachers are partners in the education of their children and that the interest, support and expertise of the one enhances parallel attitudes in the other. Levels of advice range from practical hints (TV and homework don't mix) to a quick but effective guide to the new maths.

Altogether it is a thoroughly practical booklet of easy-to-read information which, besides helping parents to make the most of their children's out-of-school experience, will also give them a glimpse of what modern primary schools are about.

Many parents will appreciate the sound advice on toys which are a good buy. It is reassuring to read the section on 'making do' which clearly states that expensive toys are not always the best or the most suitable.

Chapter six gives helpful advice on support services and sources of help on problems concerned with school, youth employment and careers.

Parents and teachers will both find something of interest here but the scope of the book is more wide-ranging than either group would require.

---

**The vital years and your child** by Audrey Bilski (Souvenir £2.50)

---

*Brenda Crowe* The strength of this book is that it is written by a woman who knows, understands and accepts mothers who want to be 'good mothers', but whose own childhood was short on 'good mothering'. She knows that nervous and physical exhaustion, poor early training in self-discipline, and an endless struggle with a small budget can lead to shouting, slapping, and scenes between husbands and wives. Parents will feel she is on their 'side', and will therefore be able to go along with her as she outlines warm, human, practical ways for parents to enrich their children's early years.

She is honest about children – the mythical 'average two-year-old' stage she describes as 'the ME and NOW phase' and adds 'socially he is hopeless!'.

Far from suggesting that parents 'teach' their children she says 'take your children out and try to see through their eyes . . .'. There is no hint of getting-children-on in the competitive sense, only endless homely examples of how parents can help themselves, as well as their children, as they live each day together.

Language and number development are seen as part – but only part – of total development; and advice on early discipline training is sane, humane and explicit as she describes how to handle the sort of fraught situations that occur between every child and his parents.

The chapter on *The first day at school* will ring a bell for most mothers. 'So keep your emotions strictly private and to yourself. Of *course* you'll feel miserable. . . . Go home then, and have a good cry and a cup of tea all to yourself in strict privacy.' Self-discipline applies to parents as well as children!

This book is to be highly recommended to those who 'know nothing about children'; and particularly to those who don't read much and will derive comfort as well as learning from the thick pages, large print, and the writer's empathy with their own feelings of inadequacy.

*Mollie Clarke* For my money this is the pick of this particular bunch. Mrs Bilski is a Froebel-trained, very experienced headmistress who has a thorough understanding of children, parents and education. She speaks with all the warmth and authority of someone who has first-hand experience of the subject in question and the ability to make herself understood by the kind of person who will read this book.

The good points which mark this book above the rest are:

1 – she gives credit to the parents and neither condescends nor harrasses. 'Fortunately God has given him superlative teachers – his parents. All they need is a little guidance and practical help which this book aims to give.'

2 – she understands young parents very well indeed and writes reassuringly about the way their dreams of parenthood give way to the reality of having a normal

noisy, destructive child. *Let's start at the beginning* is full of commonsense advice about play and communication.

3 – in underlining the importance of the highly impressionable years from two to five, she explains that everything a child sees, hears, touches, adds to his vital bank of experiences. All this is achieved without recourse to dullness or jargon. Equally sensibly, when describing points of development, she talks of stages rather than ages, which should help to prevent undue anxiety on the part of parents whose children take longer than some others to master certain crucial skills.

4 – she takes a wise middle stand between accelerated learning and the idea that no teaching of any kind should take place before school entry. This is good: 'Gradually you will build up together his own library of favourite books. If you have consistently allowed him to lead the way through his own interests and entirely voluntarily then he will taste the joys of reading and be eager for more. Then, too, he will be ready to begin to write creatively for himself.'

5 – she never loses sight of the child's basic need for encouragement and the link between learning and 'play'. Nor does she lose sight of her audience: 'The woman's mad – how can I possibly be expected to do all this and look after the baby, cook, wash, clean and shop at the same time?'

6 – perhaps Mrs Bilski's great strength is in her first-hand knowledge of modern methods, and the chapters in *Work and play* and *Education jargon* should do much to reassure and enlighten parents puzzled by current changes in classroom procedure.

Although a teacher, she has a parent's concern for the general welfare and mental health of children. 'Throughout all their lives home should be a place synonymous with warmth, security and peace – not a forcing house where they must always be striving to live up to impossibly high standards of achievement.'

# 2: EARLY READING BOOKS

## Brenda Crowe and Mollie Clarke

---

**Home-start books** by Lesley Anne Ivory; hardback cloth 45p each; limp cloth 35p each (Burke).

---

*Brenda Crowe* These books are memorable for their simplicity and beauty, and for their ability to communicate emotionally through the colouring and symmetry of the pictures. To look at them is to imagine a child on your lap, to savour the slow turning of the pages, to pause silently for the picture to be 'felt'; to hear your voice reading the simple sentences, to pause again for the picture to be seen: the child will know whether or not he wants to comment, and if he doesn't you will turn over the page serenely in order not to break the spell of togetherness. This is what pre-reading is all about, and not many books with the title *Pre-school readers* are capable of arousing this emotional and physical communication.

There will probably be many such repetitions before the child is ready to go on to the next stage of enjoyment, when he wants to talk about the pictures: and because the whole experience has been so satisfying there may come the moment when he knows the books by heart and can 'read' them aloud – but don't be fooled, he isn't reading yet, he is reciting. But it still feels good to make-believe in this way.

*Mollie Clarke* These have delightful pictures, superbly colourful with excellent use of contrast *eg* a fiery sandstorm followed by quiet night. The text is, at times, a little awkward for adult readers and (unless, by listening to adults reading the book, they know the words by heart) would certainly fox young readers. For example, try 'It is always hot and damp so the trees always have flowers and fruit' – which, additionally is a concept of vegetable growth beyond the understanding of children – and 'The tiger's stripes make him hard *to see* as he hunts in the jungle'. Really the interest and intervention of an adult will be needed if children are to have some understanding of what these attractive pictures are all about.

---

**Bright-start books** by Althea (titles include *High in the sky,* 95p; *The flower,* 95p; published by Souvenir).

---

*Brenda Crowe* These books are clear, colourful and simple but under-fives need quite a wide experience before the text and illustrations will have any meaning for them. It would be a pity to blunt the joy of books and being-read-to by putting the cart before the horse. So go shopping and buy seeds, plant them together, wait for them to grow, pick some of the flowers, wait for some to fade and turn to seed pods – then read *The flower*.

*Mollie Clarke* These books are strongly made and attractively produced with anti-dirt covers. The titles indicate appropriate books for certain occasions *eg New baby*. On the whole the pictures are bold, clear and easily identifiable although, at times, they do appear rather crude and inappropriate. It is difficult and inconsistent, for instance, for a child to be confronted with bees and butterflies which look realistic, while flowers in the same book are stylised and therefore unidentifiable.

Some of the sentences in the text are awkward and unlikely to make sense to pre-school children: 'Some men have been up and landed on the moon' and 'Perhaps they are going on business or to have a holiday in another country'. I don't find these books very appealing.

---

**First steps in reading books:** various authors (titles include *Spot and the paint, By the pool, Blackie and the wool, Rug is a bear, Rug plays tricks,* 80p each, published by Benn).

---

*Brenda Crowe* There is a stage in learning to read when a child suddenly discovers that he can actually do it! All he asks is for books that will allow him to turn page after page, while he methodically turns the black words into spoken sounds. Up to this point his teacher will have taken him slowly, with much discussion of the pictures, and casual questions designed to make sure that he understands what he reads – but at the breakthrough point there is a brief period when the mechanics of reading eclipses the desire to understand what is read.

Kathleen Brooks (*Spot and the paint, By the pool, Blackie and the wool*) clearly understands this need, and the short lines with the careful repetition of words ensures that the child will be able to press on, and on. The pictures tell the story without words, for those not yet quite ready to tackle the printed words without some idea of what it's all about.

These are not books to read aloud to children: they are essentially books for the very new reader to read aloud himself.

*Mollie Clarke* Don't accept the blurb. The illustrations are grotesquely rather than 'magnificently' eye-catching and the text 'carefully chosen' to the point of tedium reminiscent of many reading schemes. The stories are as unexciting as the text. The *Rug* books by Helen Cresswell will have greater appeal for children because most children love bears. Here again, in my opinion, the pictures are second rate and text needlessly pedestrian and repetitive.

---

**Sparks books,** various authors (titles include *A big boy hit me, My jeans, My injection, Something in my eye,* 12p each, published by Blackie).

---

*Brenda Crowe* Another series intended for children to read aloud to themselves, and most of the illustrations are an invitation to look, enjoy and ponder. But the size of the print gives pause for thought: one's eye is equally drawn to the coloured picture on the right, and the black heaviness of the print on the left.

Should the written word be quite so dominant? At this stage many children are still half-fearful of their new found ability, and those huge words seem to demand to be read rather than to suggest that they just might add to the interest of looking at the picture. They could well have this effect on parents, too, for it is sometimes assumed that big print means that the reading is easy – and that expanse of white paper is an invitation to an adult finger to point to the words one at a time, which trains pre-reading eyes badly.

Single lines have other disadvantages, too. At this stage the eye finds it difficult to 'hold' a word, turn a page, and recognise the word again immediately – repetition on the same page gives just that extra re-assurance. It just could be that this series tempts parents to try to teach their children to read, and eight years of working with backward readers and their parents have made me very wary of the pitfalls in doing it this way, with this type of book.

*Mollie Clarke* This is a very useful series. According to teachers, the books are popular with children and attractive to adults. The authors have managed to make everyday experiences interesting and significant and many of the titles will have a very therapeutic effect on apprehensive children. For pre-school children, they will provide a very useful introduction to books and a fine example of first-hand experience masquerading as second-hand experience in book form. The simplicity of the language (childlike and not tedious) will encourage early attempts at reading.

---

**Mother-and-child playbooks,** (titles include: *Let's go shopping* and *Let's go on a picnic,* 15p each, published by Young world productions).

---

*Brenda Crowe* Young world publications and the PPA collaborated on these books to try to meet the needs of children and mothers together. The idea is better than the execution: the thinking needs to evolve still further, and the illustrations leave much to be desired.

After nine years of tutoring playgroup courses, and seven years of talking with mothers up and down the country, many of us in the Pre-school Playgroups Association were very aware of the fact that mothers just don't 'see'. So it became obvious that we had to help mothers as well as children to observe, and to put their observations into words. We know too that many mothers can't read, and talk very little to their children, so that was all the more reason for helping them to communicate verbally.

We tried to plan a series of books that would challenge the powers of observation of both children and mothers (our guess was that it would often be the child who taught the mother). Mothers can become very anxious if their children aren't doing what they are supposed to be doing, so we labelled the books 'for three to five year olds' instead of 'for normal two year olds or deprived five year olds'. The books try to say that father is part of the family, and to suggest what a family might do on a non-spending-money-day-out, and also how parents can let children pack away shopping, collect objects on a walk and so on.

*Mollie Clarke* These books were prepared by the Young world publications in consultation with the Pre-school Playgroups Association. The idea is good: everyday experience reproduced as a second-hand experience in book-form. Here are all the ingredients for inculcating an interest in books *ie* familiarity with events, characters and environment. Because there is no text, mothers will have to speak to the pictures spontaneously and from their own – and therefore from their children's – experience. This kind of interchange is at the heart of language development.

Panoramic views (*eg* the supermarket) attract children and stimulate conversation and comment. The size of the book, however, is a bit too small for this kind of view and identification of the goods in the supermarket is difficult. The colours are rather crude but this is something to do with the printing.

---

**Pictures and words books** by Elizabeth Goodacre (titles include *Here is a house, On the farm,* 17p each, published by Blackie).

---

*Brenda Crowe* 'Pictures and words could tempt parents to try to teach their children to read: it is so human to want "to get them on", and these books may seem a simple way of setting about the task. But the small stereotyped illustrations offer an invitation to colour-in that is inappropriate at the pre-school stage of development. Parents would do well to leave these books alone, and to go on sharing books for their own sake, offering children a chance to paint and crayon freely on large pieces of blank paper.

*Mollie Clarke* This language – development, pre-reading scheme is illustrated (not well) in black and white and the text avoids the use of capital letters. Basically, this is for children on the brink of reading. Certainly it is for those who can grasp the shape of words. There are some ambiguities *eg* the confusion of the prepositions 'in' and 'on' appearing in a list of names and criticism can be levelled, with justice, at the house and its contents being too middle-class.

These books serve a useful purpose as language and vocabulary aids in infant classes. They will only exceptionally, I think, appeal to pre-schoolers.

---

**Book plus cassette:** *Jack and the beanstalk,* £2·95, book alone £1·35 (Holmes McDougall).

---

*Brenda Crowe* The book is a delight in its own right, with clear printing beautifully spaced on the pages, and enchanting illustrations by Bernadette Watts. The pictures are full of detail, movement and beautifully coloured. Moreover, she conveys atmosphere and uses colour, setting and expression to involve the child emotionally as the story unfolds in words and pictures. The element of fear is particularly well handled, the ogre and Jack never appear on the same page. Definitely a book to read aloud together.

So what about the tape? It was surely never intended to be a substitute for a mother's lap. I see this as an added delight at a later stage, and as such it offers several pleasures to a child fortunate enough and mature enough, to play it himself. But this should not be used as a means of getting-children-read-to, for it misses out the all important physical contact and companionship.

*Mollie Clarke* The book is reasonably attractive and convincing although the beanstalk looks a bit too insubstantial for climbing. Mother's reaction to the sight of the loot, 'She was very pleased' seems like a particularly bad anti-climax.

*Jack and the beanstalk* on cassette is very well told and the quality of the man's voice suits the story. The going up and going down music is a good beginning to musical interpretation and the harp comes sweetly into its own at the end of the cassette. It all makes an intimate experience.

---

**Storycards and picture map:** *A day in the country* by Sally Cedar (Jonathan Cape 95p).

---

*Brenda Crowe* What a beautiful present for the right child! One of our children would have adored it, understood it, and played with it for talkative hours at the age of four years. The other child would have enjoyed picking out the pictures at random and saying '. . . now tell me about that one!' She would also have enjoyed tracing a route with her finger and saying 'Tell me about this house!' – but if I had produced a card saying 'This tells you what is happening in that house' she would have refuted it utterly.

*Mollie Clarke* The unusual format is attractive with a wallet containing nine storycards and a map of the imaginary village of Turley. Text is 'engrossing and instructive'. However, this does present a fairly formidable problem and would be more appropriate for eight year olds and older – particularly those who are beginning to think about maps, scale and the function of working communities.

# 3: PRE-SCHOOL KITS

## Brenda Crowe and Mollie Clarke

Dona Haycraft

**The teach your baby to read kit** by Glenn Doman (Cape, £2.50) with **Teach your baby to read** by Glenn Doman (Cape £1.95)

*Brenda Crowe* If I had a brain-damaged child I would make a beeline for Dr Doman, trusting not only in his skill and experience but in his ability to give me hope, confidence and guidance. In earlier times I would likewise have sought out Madame Montessori, who also combined medical skill, insight and sensitivity.

I don't believe we can afford the risk involved in adopting the teaching of any one person, however dedicated, brilliant, successful and loving he may be, without asking *Why?* and going on to ask searching questions about ourselves as parents (which we are unlikely to be able to answer honestly since we are emotionally involved).

If we accept the fact that babies can learn to read, and if we shelve for the moment the vital question 'do we want them to?' we would still need to ask the question 'from whom?'.

Dr Doman would say from me and my team, or through my book. But he cannot afford to overlook this vital fact: it is irresponsible to imagine that mothers in isolation can go and buy a book and a teaching kit and do the job as he would have it done.

For his passionate conviction and enthusiasm blinds him to the implication of what he is saying, and some of his statements need to be thought through in more detail. To take one example: the seven-year-old 'teacher' who succeeded in teaching all her three and five year olds to read the vocabulary of 25 words that she gave them was 'playing'. Fine, and the children learned through their play – but their emotional relationship with their seven-year-old friend wasn't in the least like their relationship with their mothers. They could have gone home whenever they liked, and not gone back: they could have left her and gone *to* their mothers for comfort or relief from pressure: it is unlikely that the 'teacher' gave the exaggerated response of pride and joy to each child, at each success, that the mother is advised to give – and in the face of mother's emotional reaction it would be difficult for her child to accept that she was 'only playing' as the children knew themselves to be.

*Mollie Clarke* The first part of the book describes the development of reading skills in brain-damaged and/or very young children. The real dichotomy occurs when the 'success' of these young children (mainly in reading) is compared with the development of 'normal' children whose learning (information and skills) covers a much wider field. To quote Doman: '. . . the foregoing does not prove that brain-injured children are superior to normal children, but simply that normal children are not achieving what they can and *should*.'

His method rests entirely on the use of prepared flash cards with large-size (because young children have difficulty in seeing small print) eye-catching scarlet letters. The words are those which are important ones in the life of any child. The first step, for instance, consists of the recognition of two words, 'mummy and daddy'.

The text explains, in great detail, how this approach builds up to sentence construction and use of a first reading book.

Perhaps the most significant chapter of all is the one on joyousness. Doman lists basic dos and don'ts. But given that parents have the attitudes and interests described here, most children flourish in any aspect of learning whatever methods are employed. In any close, one-to-one parent-child relationship it is difficult to separate the emotional and cognitive gains. It is doubtful, however, if all this can be guaranteed for the price of the kit and it would be interesting to know how many attempts on the part of enthusiastic parents and obedient children have had, eventually, to be discarded. If so, one is unlikely to be able to assess the damage as easily as Doman describes the successes of the system.

**The parents' guidance kit for the under fives** by John Godwin (Cressrelles, £4.25)

*Brenda Crowe* John Godwin writes with simplicity, commonsense, sensitivity and a clear concern for the overall happiness and joy that he sees as the essence of the parent/child relationship, and the basis of all learning.

He wisely states his aims, and his manual and kit are intended '. . . for the needs of children who are not underprivileged in homes where the parents are not without education'. He further says: 'I am assuming that mothers who wish to give their children positive educational help . . . have themselves a love of books and of reading, together with a good grasp of correctly spoken English. I am also assuming that they are emotionally capable of embarking upon this educational adventure in an atmosphere which is happy, and where the child is entirely free from undue stress and strain . . .'

My feeling is that the practical suggestions are so good and possible that, with even more everyday examples, the manual would stand alone without those parts relating to the kit, and the kit itself.

From WHERE 99 (December 1974)

Sorting nuts, buttons and sweets: playing Snap and Happy families; learning to hear and interpret such sounds as saucepans boiling over, dustbin lids clattering, letters on the mat, is the very stuff of family life. The suggested remarks, questions and guessing games can be recognised and adapted to our many cultures. The art of mothering needs to be revived, and this book stirs the imagination for those who haven't such warm childhood memories to guide them.

Educational firms now supply such attractive, strong and varied materials for sorting, grading, matching, naming, that it seems a pity to offer children the materials in the kit – card bends so easily, and is so frustrating and unsatisfactory once it is no longer immaculate.

*Mollie Clarke* The 96-page guide is written modestly and with some diffidence and John Godwin knows much about what he is doing to underline three cautionary points – (*1*) the emotional climate between child and parent-teacher must be right (*2*) at no time must child or parent feel threatened or under stress (*3*) no kit can do everything: real life experiences are essential.

He makes no bones about the fact that he is not writing for the benefit of children from underprivileged homes but for children of 'average to superior intelligence' from a reasonably well-endowed background.

He uses the language of learning and development with all the assurance of an experienced qualified teacher and many parents will be impressed with the threefold objective of the kit – (*1*) visual discrimination (*2*) ability to classify (*3*) capacity for hand-eye co-ordination.

The material is small and fiddly and the preparation of the cards and their eventual dismantling would pose a quite considerable task for busy mothers. Parents are advised to employ ingenuity and imagination in their use of these materials.

---

**Training in basic cognitive skills** (10 booklets £1.22 each; handbook 59p); **Training in motor skills** (10 booklets £1.09 each; handbook 59p), by Margaret Paull and Simon Haskell (ESA)

---

*Brenda Crowe* Once again work with handicapped children has led to a series of booklets planned to help the development of normal children. The planning and presentation of the booklets is clear and beautifully uncluttered, it is unusual to find such generosity of paper and so much space round the well placed exercises. This is important for so much that is offered to children is small, cramped and ungenerous.

The accompanying manual would be difficult for many parents to read, let alone understand ('children should be given extensive opportunity to isolate the common and unique instances of objects and events in their environment') but the instructions for each page are specific and natural ('one could say: the snail wants to crawl along to the crocus. You try to draw the path he takes. He goes slowly, and he must not bump against the sides of the path.').

It is easy to imagine the delight and satisfaction of a child at school, or a child from a 'good mothering' home, 'playing' with a relaxed and happy adult. I would have welcomed the set to hide away for a rainy day, a visit to the out-patients department, convalescence, or a visit to a home not geared to children. With a minimum of friendly comment the children could have carried out simple tasks with pride, joy and success, without having any idea that they were being-done-good-to. Full marks for this.

But to suggest, as the publishers do, that this series is suitable for playgroup leaders is to misunderstand completely the nature of the playgroup movement.

*Mollie Clarke* The introductory sections on cognitive development and play are useful at any level. The eight booklets concerned with motor development (pre-writing) take the child through an organised sequence of the simpler components of writing activity until mastery of writing proper is achieved.

The interest of the exercise depends on the ingenuity and imagination of the parent in the way she introduces the activities and pictures to her child.

These booklets may give some kind of pleasure and confidence to parent and child. But there are limitations: the difficult labour of going over all those dotted lines could produce cramped and tense control and a strong dislike of paper and pencil. Sugar paper, large crayons and free drawing will produce (in the long run) better results.

---

**The three four five nursery course** by Iris Grender (Three four five Ltd £11·75)

---

*Brenda Crowe* In spite of the sincerity and affection for children, which clearly inspired the author to produce this course, it misses the mark on so many counts.

There is a dreadful monotony in the illustrations: all 12 books are filled with the same lifeless symbols of people, animals and objects.

There is inbuilt frustration in any cardboard models that are intended to lie flat together, or stand up firmly. As I tried to press out the shapes (very few came out perfectly) and fold and slot the buildings, old childhood memories flooded back with full force – together with memories of our own children trying to cope with the same apparently simple but exasperating tasks. As fast as you slot one end in, the other end pops out, and if mother does it, what's the point?

So many of the assumptions are doubtful. Would sticky tape on the joins of the models really enable children to 'play vigorously' with them? Do under-fives really enjoy a trip to a museum or a stately home? Is it fair to suggest that the poor mother makes this expensive trip (in cash, time and energy) while at the same time warning her that the visit must be short?

There is a coyness that jars. The parents who need help over sex education will eagerly agree that the first question is often 'what's this hole in my tummy?' But it doesn't help to be told 'just answer each question as it comes'. The 64-dollar question is indeed 'how does the baby get into mummy's tummy?' but it's not playing fair to say 'swallow hard and blurt it out'. Blurt precisely *what* out?

The overall feeling is one of stifling smallness and be-carefulness: lines to trace, fiddly things to match, questions to answer that could so much more profitably have been asked in the natural communication of everyday living. Everything seems to need such care and control, and yet not to be worthy of the effort involved.

Those who would welcome support like this need help of a different kind not offered in this course.

*Mollie Clarke* This is a beguilingly attractive set of fairly expensive, well-heeled comics, with sections for mummy, daddy and the record-player. For those children whose parents have the necessary money and leisure, the course can only do good. Whether the one-to-one attention and pleasurable rapport produces the benefits or whether the materials themselves are responsible is an academic point. There is no doubt they would enhance the pre-school experience of any child as would any contact with rhymes, games, stories and creative activity.

Two final comments: if this course is to cover a year, there does not seem to me to be enough progression in the cognitive demands in the child participator. Secondly, the 'fringe' activities could be more imaginative, more linked to another interest in the same volume and cover a wider field. Interest in the environment (real as opposed to the imaginary village) could be included – especially biological interests.

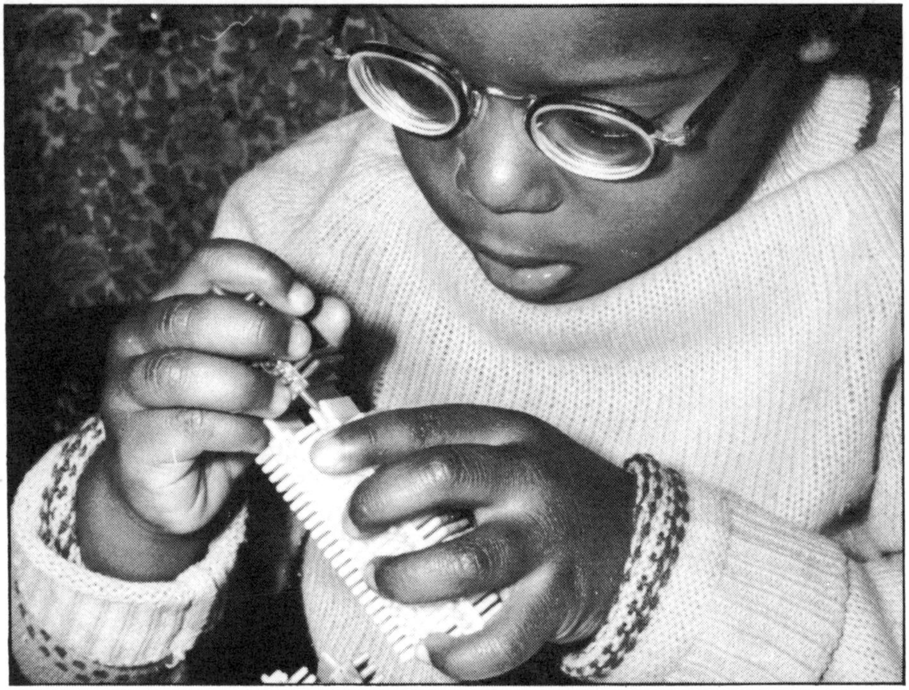
Bob Bray

# 4: BOOKS ON PRACTICAL ACTIVITIES FOR PARENTS AT HOME WITH THEIR PRE-SCHOOL CHILDREN

## Brenda Crowe, Mollie Clarke and Joanna Matthews

**Day-by-day learning books** (titles are *Numbers, Opposites, Time* and *The alphabet,* Hamlyn, 95p each)

*Brenda Crowe* These books are beautifully illustrated, bound and presented – I would love to share them with children on this score alone, particularly for the pleasure of the colouring, texture and design of the pictures. What of the learning? The books vary, and even with the different books adult expectations of learning will vary – best really just to enjoy the books together, and the chances are that the children's enjoyment will take them back to the books a sufficient number of times for their learning from experience to begin to be linked to the subject matter of the books.

The sentence in *Time* 'The first division of time is a second . . .' means nothing, but 'It takes a second to wink an eye or to burst a balloon – it takes a second for a soldier to bang a drum' is both interesting and challenging.

*Mollie Clarke* As a publishing exercise these colourful, attractively bound books represent reasonably good value for money at 65p each. Each book is illustrated by a different artist.

The semi-stylised, elaborately patterned pictures in the *Alphabet* vary in quality and clarity of purpose. They are, however, colourful and pleasantly textured and mother and child will enjoy hunting down the objects named against each letter of the alphabet.

As an aid to early readers and writers it will be less useful because of the limitation of space (maximum of six words on one page) and the choice of nouns.

*Time* from the content point of view, is a winner. It looks at time from a child's point of view and relates short and longer periods of time to everyday experience. Information about clocks and watches is interesting and ideas about day and night, the days of the week and the months and seasons of the year are gradually introduced without too much artificiality. The text is well and suitably written and the illustrations appropriate and pleasing.

These books will never appear on lists of recommended literature for pre-school children. They are, however, considerably better than many more expensively priced books. Not a bad buy.

*Joanna Matthews* I particularly enjoyed Mike Ricketts' *Numbers*. This is as much a story of animals on a farm through the day, as it is a counting book, and yet there's no text. The illustrator has an understanding of an animal's characteristics. I fell for the starey-eyed kittens as much as I do for real kittens, and his goat eats the numbers.

*Opposites* by Ken Astrop is more of a mixture. Some very imaginative new ways of illustrating contrasting ideas, like 'whisper' and 'shout', boys 'asleep' and boys 'awake' pillow-fighting, 'hard' seaside candy rock and 'soft' ice-cream. But there are also some tired old clichés and some doggerel verse. No explanations of how a book like this works, just a take-it-or-leave-it presentation, and the assumption that it is a helpful approach and in many ways this is enough.

---

**Learning with mother books 1–5** by E. and H. Wingfield (Ladybird, 24p each)

---

*Brenda Crowe* A delightful series illustrating yet again that it's 'not what you do but the way that you do it' that matters. The illustrations show so clearly that it is the quality of relationships that matters above all else; there are grannies and grandads, fathers and mothers with the children – all believable people, wearing believable clothes and hairstyles, some with glasses, some plump, some slender, some with engagement rings as well as wedding rings. There is a wealth of detail yet the overall impression is one of simplicity – and the constantly reiterated implication is that play can be absorbing to adults, especially to mothers who have to combine children and chores. These books show how to combine caring for the children and the home in such a way that the two jobs complement each other.

Parents who have few memories of time shared with their own parents often need help if they are to create a different family pattern with their own children. These books offer help over those aspects of mothering that don't always come naturally. For example, book three says on nearly every page 'discuss the picture with your child. *Be a good listener to anything your child might wish to say.*'

What is more, the pictures really do invite conversation because the children, parents, activities and settings are so life-like. This is a valuable and attractive series.

*Mollie Clarke* These five books serve a dual-purpose. For parents, they provide a simple, but useful, guide to the main stages of child development besides offering a host of essentially practical suggestions for enhancing the right kind of pre-school learning. For children, they provide picture/discussion material conveniently linked to everyday interests.

At £1.20 for the set of five, these books certainly give value for money. There is something here for any parent who is prepared to read the text carefully and go to the trouble of trying out some of the many ideas and techniques. Book 1 covers the first two years and books 2–5 each deal with a one-year range from two to five. The material contained in each book is reassuringly appropriate for the age group concerned and the parent is gently led from early sensory learning to preliminary contact with the child's first school. The suggested activities link directly with children's environmental discoveries and the maximum use is made of inexpensive and easily obtained materials.

*Joanna Matthews* A simple format, one page of text opposite a coloured picture for each topic. Mother is encouraged to do things with her child, with the emphasis on conversation and using what is to hand. Much is conveyed by detail in the illustrations, like sharing with dad and grandmother the learning stages of the family. The child learns to assimilate much experience by playing through it on his own terms. Pretending is not escape, but part of the work of learning.

---

**Ladybird playbooks 1 and 2** by E. and H. Wingfield (Ladybird, 24p each)

---

*Brenda Crowe* Ethel and Harry Wingfield write as though they do care about, and understand, parents as well as children, and this is all too rare. The result is that they don't make the mistake of assuming that all parents have happy memories of being cuddled up on laps whilst being read to: they seem to accept quite naturally and easily that many parents love their children dearly and want to do their best for them, but may not know where to begin.

This is a work-book format, and the follow-up suggestions are simple, practical and possible.

One of the great strengths of these books is that although the authors clearly know precisely what they hope the child will learn from each page, *they don't let the reader in on it* – if they did the fun could so easily give way to earnestness, and it is the naturalness of the parent/child relationship that is so valuable.

*Mollie Clarke* These are large, attractively arranged books at the astonishingly low cost of 24p.

On the left hand side of each spread, are clear instructions for the parent; on the right hand side is a picture which poses an interesting problem for the child. Each page has a high but appropriate language content and many opportunities for the child to

From WHERE 101/102 (February/March 1975)

R. A. Batt

become involved in the situation.

Above all, there is the fringe (but highly significant) advantage of good communication and inter-relation between child and parent. Very good value indeed – how do they do it?

*Joanna Matthews* These are low priced and expendable and have much to offer. Good activities with dough, and a new dimension in bracelets made by cutting across sealed up old envelopes. It's a pity that some of the cutting out needed to make the sorting games come on the back of the other games. The introduction emphasises that a positive effort must be made not to instil a sense of urgency and need for achievement into the learning process at this age. These books are for the end of the pre-school period, younger ones will find that mother has to do too much for them and the play value is lost.

---

**You can draw the seaside** by Brian Paine (Cressrelles, 80p)

---

*Brenda Crowe* This book is a complete denial of the creativity of children, and shows a total lack of understanding of child development. Parents encouraging their children to copy these symbols will inhibit natural development, and will literally do more harm than good.

*Mollie Clarke* This book will curl the hair of all those concerned with art education in the past 20 years. It sets out, shamelessly, to teach children how to draw certain objects by using straight and curved lines. Even the use of these lines is not left to the child's imagination as each object is drawn step by step for the child to copy. The results of this method are deplorable. Waves behave as water never has, sand castles have ruler-straight edges, one-armed and one-legged mothers and fathers lounge on deck chairs with no seats.

*Joanna Matthews* Part of the literature of stereotype and cliché, this gives instructions on how to draw pin-men, waves and castles with accurate pot-hooks more suited to learning shorthand than to encouraging expressiveness and learning about the world.

---

**Help your child at home books** by John Akers (titles are *The birthday party* and *Mary and Mike go shopping* at 12½p each; *The starting school alphabet book* and *The starting school number book* at 62½p each; Caversham)

---

*Brenda Crowe* These sort of books, especially when intended for the under-fives, concentrate on the getting-ready-for-school stage without seeming to see childhood as a state in its own right. They also assume that parents and children are already enjoying each other in a warm and spontaneous relationship – those parents who are need no books of this type: those who aren't need help to see that relaxed enjoyment of the parent/child/book stage is the best possible help that they can give before school.

*Mollie Clarke* These books will do children no harm. In the sense that they demand a high degree of communication between parent and child they may make a considerable contribution towards the child's general development in ways that the author had not foreseen. It is doubtful if any child will get more than superficial gains from this pleasant but unexciting academic activity. Only pre-school children who have had considerable previous experience in looking at books, handling crayons and scissors will be able to tackle the activities without a great deal of help.

It is perhaps unnecessary to point out that beamed cafés, birthday parties and school uniforms are not part of every child's daily life. But then not every child will handle these books.

*Joanna Matthews* Two of these short illustrated books are about a birthday party and going shopping for school uniform. Both are fairly solid stereotype and the books themselves won't stand comparison with other more recent multi-coloured illustrated books. 'Starting school alphabet' and 'Starting school number book' are more like colouring-in books. I liked the rows of houses, some with missing numbers, odd down one side of the street, and even along the other. But the text is unappealing to the eye, and you might well find yourself skipping the adult's part.

---

**Busy books 1–6** (Collins, 90p for the six)

---

*Brenda Crowe* The simple and direct instructions in these books are aimed straight at the children, with no notes to parents, so it can be taken (one hopes) that the children will be free to accept or reject them. If this is so, there will be a stage when many just-readers will probably delight in them – which of us can't remember going through a workbook (that was well within our grasp) with the feeling of satisfaction as we completed each page and turned to the next? If the books are used to *teach* reading, then the whole object of the exercise will have been missed: these books are to reinforce the lovely feeling of 'I can do that . . . and that . . . and that!' The spaces left for the child's illustrations are realistically large, and it is nice to have a whole blank page for 'Anything you like'.

A word of warning: the progression of assumed learning is steep – if book 1 has been enjoyed on a wet Monday, it is highly unlikely that book 5 will be similarly enjoyed on Friday.

*Mollie Clarke* These are cheaply produced

R. A. Batt

(and unlike the Ladybird series they look cheap) work books of the traditional type. Each book combines practice in reading, writing, comprehension, colouring and drawing. Some children would enjoy using them on a wet day or during a period of convalescence. There is nothing about any book in the series which would stimulate a child to further activity or self-initiated tasks.

*Joanna Matthews* Six instalments of directives on poor quality paper, much of which is blank so the child can draw what he is instructed: 'Draw a picture story about a present'. There is no text to justify these commands, no coherent theory. This is slavery, and a sure way to lose imagination and gain nothing instead.

---

**Starting points** edited by Henry Pluckrose (titles include *Let's paint, Let's make a picture, Let's model with plaster, Let's build;* Evans, 60p each)

---

*Brenda Crowe* These are not for the under-fives, since they are written directly to the children who will be reading them – which is fine. The layout is clear, the directions natural and minimal, and the illustrations of children's work ring true.

It is good to see books that aim to start children off on their own explorations – the parent is not required to 'teach', only to offer the friendship and work space that will enable the child to do his own learning and enjoying.

*Mollie Clarke* This series will be used by children of seven or eight years onwards and most of the techniques would be too advanced for pre-school children. But the illustrations are reproductions of children's work and are particularly attractive.

*Joanna Matthews* These are aimed at school-age children. But many of the techniques *are* adaptable for under-fives. For the pre-school child it is the process itself, the creative work that counts, the finished object is of much less concern.

*Let's paint* has a lot of useful information about materials, but the instructions are much too directive in many cases. I was disappointed in the finger painting. To use fingers as if they were substitute brushes does not release the full power of this technique. Small children like to build up a rhythm using their whole bodies, with all of both hands working in the paint.

*Let's make a picture* Watch out for the age of the children. The illustrations are children's work, you can just see their hands in the small photos. Round about eight perhaps. This gets away from the idea of paint as the only medium for pictures. *Let's model in plaster* is almost entirely for older children.

I'd like to add *Let's build* by Rita Davies which gets away from the flat object and introduces three dimension to which many children, especially boys, seem to react with interest. The materials needed are mostly scrap, which is very useful.

---

**You can make it books** prepared in consultation with Henry Pluckrose (titles include *Pictures, Toys, Models, Gifts;* Nelson, 25p each)

---

*Brenda Crowe* These are disappointing after Henry Pluckrose's editing of *Starting points* for whereas the latter series was, literally, a series of starting points, the *'You can make it'* books are a depressing series of end-products. This is all the more worrying as the illustrations indicate that they are intended for the younger children, and there is real danger that parents and others will deny children their much-needed period of personal exploration and experiment with raw materials in favour of 'helping them to make things'.

It can't be said often enough that the desire for an end-product is very rare in young children, it is the 'doing' that matters. And the paper boats, eggbox tanks, toilet-roll binoculars, and peg and pipecleaner grasshoppers offered in these books are a sad reflection on society's lack of understanding of how children develop their skills and imagination through undirected play.

*Mollie Clarke* In *Pictures* the activities move from the transient pleasures of making patterns and pictures with flour and cereals to the more permanent satisfaction of cutting and sticking pictures. This is a colourful and attractively set out book which will interest children. The picture directions are so obvious they will have no difficulty in trying out the techniques.

*Models* is most attractively designed with good photography, well-printed labels and interesting, if limited, ideas.

On balance, this is an attractive series and one which will have immediate appeal for parents and children. It is a pity that the examples produced are not more original and exciting.

*Joanna Matthews* Glossily illustrated, with barely any words at all. Very attractive to the eye, but I am sorry that almost all the illustrations look as if they are adults' work. The mother without experience of what three or four year olds can produce would get no help from these. And mother and child will be disappointed if they try to reproduce the illustrations. It could end up with mother doing everything and child feeling a failure. Having said that, I did like some of the ideas in *Models*. A sand garden and a lighthouse on the beach with real sand and shells. But next to it a cliché rabbit, plainly made out of the inside of a toilet roll, prudishly called a 'cardboard tube'. A mixed bag, mostly not my flavour.

CCAT

**Mother's help** edited by Susan Dickinson (Collins, £1·95; Fontana 50p)

*Brenda Crowe* I can't really comment on a book to which I have contributed, but perhaps I may explain how it was written.

The title of the book is true twice over. The contributors are all aware of the strains and stresses involved in looking after young children and a home all day and every day. They offer suggestions to help mothers to meet their own need for a manageable day, and their children's need for play in the real sense of that miraculous word. But it is also a book that tries to show that children can be a real help to their mothers: they really can cook! Mothers come to understand, through working together, just how capable and companionable their children can be: the relationship between them alters from mother-looks-after-child to one of real friendship – she still looks after him, but then don't we always look after our friends?

*Mollie Clarke* This is a comprehensive guide to good play-grouping for mothers and leaders who have little time for more profound reading and study. A quick glance at the list of collaborators is totally reassuring. Here we have well-known names, such as Brenda Crowe, Eileen Colwell and Moira Keenan, experts in many fields who happen at the same time, to be thoroughly familiar with the mountains and molehills of preschooling. Fairly and squarely it adjusts our perspective and underlines priorities. To take just one example, Eileen Colwell wastes no words in introducing her excellent comprehensive book list. In four pages she summarises, rather brilliantly, the different types of stories, their construction and their appeal, and underlines what should be our main considerations when selecting and telling (or reading) stories.

There is also excellent, reliable advice on supporting the mental and psychological health of physically sick children. The sections on hospitalised children and accidents are particularly useful.

*Joanna Matthews* This is a collection of pieces by various authors for 'busy mothers and playgroup leaders'. Music, dressing-up, art and creative activities, cooking, parties, or the child in bed – these may be areas in which mothers feel at a loss, with some level of anxiety, minor maybe, but enough to undermine their feeling of adequacy to cope. Here is the help they crave.

**Not yet five** by Gwenda Bartram (ESA, 97p)

*Brenda Crowe* This is another book for parents who aren't too sure what to suggest when children say 'What can I do?'. Even if it occurred to some to make a house under the kitchen table by putting a rug over the top, it may well not have occurred to them that in between household tasks they could 'pretend to be "auntie" with her new baby, or nana, or Mrs Brown coming to visit'.

The section on junk is marred by suggestions of 'things to make' – if the various cartons, containers, materials and glue or paste are attractively set out for children they will do their own experimenting and discovering. Parents need to be encouraged to learn from watching their children; they will find that what is created is likely to be delightfully crazy and unrecognisable, but that the satisfaction on the child's face is proof of its worth to him. Adults need to see the world through a child's eyes.

An otherwise good section on painting is also marred by offering parents the stereotyped symbols for a house, car, and back view of a cat as suitable illustrations for a story. While we continue handing down to children these visual clichés we shall make it more difficult for them to use their own imagination with confidence.

It is the home-centred, mother and child centred, learning that is the strength of this book.

*Mollie Clarke* This is essentially an ideas book and like many such books it achieves shape without substance. In something which attempts to give advice affecting children, this can be dangerous. The brief notes and explanations make it quite clear that the author has fallen into the trap of differentiating between activities with 3Rs potential and play for enjoyment and social experience. Basically the idea is to try out certain tricks and techniques on pre-school children and find out if they catch on: if not, the author advises patience and second attempts at a later date. There is nothing here about finding the right (intellectually and psychologically) moment for introducing new ideas and little about allowing children, in a well prepared environment, to stumble for themselves on some of these activities.

The section on the development of drawing is both dogmatic and superficial. There's more to it than appears here and it would be a pity if parents begin to worry about the rate of transfer from wavy to circular scribble.

The sections on sorting, matching, discriminating and counting could provide a useful guide for those who want to make this kind of equipment. As this kind of activity operates in a fairly structured field, the descriptions leave no one in a quandary.

*Joanna Matthews* The author gives a fair coverage of activities in the pre-reading and pre-writing skills. Using a sort of shopping list style, this leads to rather more directive than explanation. The emphasis is on extension of vocabulary and looking at things. The five senses are given scant reference, and the sense of smell, that fastest-vanishing of all the senses so acute in children, is ignored. Water-play here is for learning to measure, not for the joy of pouring over and over again. No emotional life is hinted at, a factor which is so critical in learning.

---

**Playing, learning and living** by Vera Roberts (Black, £1·50)

---

*Brenda Crowe* Vera Roberts' book is full of vitality and happiness. She is not just doing-children-good, she is enjoying herself as part of the bargain.

Her attitude to deprivation is a welcome change from some of the current ideas on 'compensatory education': 'Children from a restricted background need the experiences which are the very stuff of everyday life – making tea, sweeping, washing up, cooking, and so on, and they need an adult to talk to them about the work in hand, and to recall it afterwards. *They need what has aptly been described as "mental companionship".*'

She puts communication before language, and understands that there are times when silence is the best possible means of communication.

She doesn't take herself too seriously, and tells how a fidgety three-year-old listened (apparently) to a well-told story with flattering attention, only to say at the end: 'You've got a silver tooth.'

If I was asked to recommend books to mothers who want to help their children, but aren't too sure how to go about it, this would be one of them.

*Mollie Clarke* Vera Roberts is the well-known and respected headmistress of a famous nursery school in London. She writes with all the authority of one who has practised what she preaches with children for over 30 years.

In 19 chapters she covers most of the main responsibilities confronting those who work with pre-school children. A glance at the index shows that this is a thoroughly practical book and no major issue has been ducked.

The chapter headed 'keeping your head above water', shows that she is an expert at spotting situations likely to rock the pre-school boat. At the same time, she has lost nothing of her dedication to the cause of early childhood education and the references to actual children and real situations which occur throughout the book show that her main concern is that of ensuring good conditions for the development of children.

*Joanna Matthews* Written to help the nursery teacher, any parent would understand what goes on in a nursery class after reading the descriptions of equipment and activities, which are based on many years experience. Parents may be a bit hurt to find they are not included in the chapter on working with other adults, but rather have a chapter to themselves on *problems*, which include sleeping and feeding difficulties, toilet training and sex instruction, all taken as out-of-school problems.

---

**Playgroup activities** by Brenda Crowe (Pre-school Playgroups Association, 60p)

---

*Brenda Crowe* Clearly I am in no position to comment on this. It came to be written after several years of tutoring playgroup courses during which I became aware of the jargon barrier between me and the mothers. They couldn't connect what I was saying about children's play needs with their own ability to meet these needs in their homes and playgroups – hence a book written from the home-centred parent angle rather than the nursery school teacher's angle.

*Mollie Clarke* This is a book for playgroupers at all levels written by their national adviser in her own racy and amusing style. There is no doubt, however, about her sheer professionalism. In spite of the limitations of a book of this kind and at this price, she manages to underline all the essentials, point out priorities, issue worthwhile caveats and, at the same time, achieve instant rapport with the readers by including warm, human anecdotes.

*Joanna Matthews* About what goes on in a playgroup, it is about the children and the adults. The only book of the bunch that gives any description of what mothers feel about what their children do, and what we do to our children. Children need to play with the basic materials of our world, including sand, water and clay, but many children react as if using these messy materials was 'naughty', and they need to learn how to cope with them, and with the often confusing adult rules imposed on them.

Equipment and technique are described for each activity, as well as the overall planning of a session. Beginners always want to get down to it, and can't wait to begin, so there is a quick run-through initially, and a later deeper look into each activity, plus a most perceptive and realistic discussion of how the various adults in the playgroup relate to one another and to the children.

---

**Pre-school activities** by Dorothy and John Pickering (Batsford, £2.10)

---

*Brenda Crowe* The title of this book belies the beauty and vision locked away between the covers. The overworked word 'activities' takes on a new meaning because of the quality of wonder, delight and awareness that permeates the very stuff of living – for the authors.

Movement – the wiggling of toes, the movement of faces and tongues that produces different sounds, the movement of real feathered wings (not arms flapping up and down and called wings), the movement of wind on faces and blowing through hair, the movement of tall grasses as a child trudges through them.

Lines, not just lines on paper but wet tricycle tyres on dry cement, a wet brush on a dry fence, the lines on leaves, wood, feathers, 'vapour trails, plough furrows, and water channels to the sea'. Not lines to be 'taught', but lines to be seen, experienced, shared, enjoyed, just for their own sake and as part of the experience of living.

Shapes – to be stroked, climbed-over, grasped; moving shapes, hard and soft shapes, shapes to be explored with the whole body as the child gets in, under and through.

Holes – 'The reasons why children dig holes are somewhat obscure but it seems obvious that they find it enjoyable. . . .' Hooray!

*Mollie Clarke* This is a refreshingly unusual book and one which brings the reader firmly into the pre-school child's world. The authors are professional educationalists in colleges of education. John Pickering's expertise in the field of visual education accounts for the superb photographs which accompany the elegant text.

The theme of the book is particularly attractive:

> Although there are many new materials available and the range and quality are vast and varied, it should be possible to create exciting situations and stimulate children with extremely simple things . . . it will succeed if it acts as no more than a catalyst in helping teachers to look again with fresh eyes at ways of encouraging a child in his power of discrimination and response to the environment.

Sections of the book deal with different kinds of sensory experience, sight, hearing, touch and bodily movement and there are many delightful photographs of children to illustrate the points the authors want to stress. Ever since Montessori we have been talking about the need for children to learn through the senses, to develop sensory awareness. This book helps to shift the focus, giving us a clearer view of the unparalleled value of everyday experiences. It is a shot in the arm for rut-dwellers.

*Joanna Matthews* This is a complete contrast to *Not yet five*. The cover picture is of a child playing shapes with his shadow. A child pours dry sand over his bare tummy. Here are children learning through their senses. Activities are connected by words like 'movement' and 'line'. Children step by step are making sense out of the booming, buzzing universe.

---

**Pre-school play** by Kenneth Jameson and Pat Kidd (Studio Vista, £1·95)

---

*Brenda Crowe* Kenneth Jameson is an artist who loves children: he became fascinated by the work that children did in nursery schools and playgroups, and the birth of his first granddaughter heightened his awareness of the difficulties that many parents find in providing for their young children's play needs at home. Pat Kidd is a teacher who became deeply involved with playgroups, and playgroup courses, when her own children were at the playgroup age.

The authors took their own photographs, and there are ideas for everyone – a child crouched in a 'house' made from plastic milk bottle crates; one in the garden ladling soap froth from a washing-up bowl into a saucepan; a small group in a backyard carefully dismantling a discarded television set (we are told how to render it safe first); a sweeper-upper enchanted by the brush trails on the paving stones; a small charmer marvelling at herself in the mirror as the sun sparkles on the tinsel strand that she holds against her hair; a home corner created by cotton curtains designed to slip over the backs of a row of kitchen chairs.

The great strength of this book is that it offers innumerable bridges between children's needs and the parents who would so gladly meet them if only they knew how. It is written by parents, for parents, on behalf of children.

*Mollie Clarke* With both Kenneth Jameson, ILEA adviser, and Pat Kidd, senior professional adviser for the Inner London Pre-school Playgroups Association, this book should be a winner. For extra strength, David Evans, schools' music adviser to ILEA, has contributed a section on early musical experiences.

In fact, what they have produced is a well-presented and useful summary of basic pre-school activities with reliable details of relevant materials and techniques. It is a sort of mini-encyclopaedia of pre-school play arranged under some two dozen headings which embrace everything from fantasy to fiddle boards. Each section includes sound practical advice on the selection of equipment, organisation of materials, the natural development of skills and the right kind of intervention on the part of the adult. There is nothing here to cause stress or anxiety; on the contrary, the book is infinitely reassuring and helpful.

*Joanna Matthews* A great wealth of experience from the authors is passed on in practical and understanding ways. They point to the much wider range of the imaginative and creative needs of very young children. In the, inevitably, brief explanations of each activity, I missed the ex-

Dona Haycraft

panded wisdom of Jameson's own book on children's painting *(Pre-school and infant art* Studio Vista, £2·75). The setting here is the playgroup. So read and enjoy it, much can be used just as effectively and pleasurably at home.

---

**Trumper's playgroup book** by Delphine Evans (Blackie, £1·50)

---

*Brenda Crowe* The title is misleading, since almost the only reference to playgroups is the toy elephant's coy 'Can you guess what else I do? I belong to a playgroup just like you', followed by the depressing picture of Trumper's mum abandoning him in one, with a curt 'Goodbye, see you later'. We have a brief and equally depressing glimpse of Mrs Cherry ringing a bell for lunch and everybody sitting in a circle for the register – poor Trumper.

It is impossible to escape the conclusion that this title and opening gambit, plus a story about a Tufty club, are a bid to attract a market for a book of stories, rhymes and finger-plays that would have little appeal on its own merits.

*Mollie Clarke* This is a rag-bag of a book and, like all rag-bags it throws up bits of varying quality and usefulness.

The basic idea that a child will learn to tolerate the burden of pre-school or playgroup life by seeing her problems transferred to her toy elephant is simple, obvious and psychologically sound. In my opinion, we could have done with rather more of Trumper and rather less of the jingles and finger-plays. Here again, these vary in quality but, in general they hit a low literary level and are too complicated for easy memorisation by children and adults.

The idea of finger-puppets fascinates all children and it is a pity that these stories are fairly pedestrian. The chatty episodic nature of the book closely resembles *The Archers* and, like that programme, it makes too-obvious attempts to introduce new ideas and cautionary tales – 'As I expect you know, elephants usually live in hot lands', 'You know it's dangerous to go near fireworks', 'As everybody knows, it is very dangerous to go near a hot cooker'.

At the present time, we have to look carefully at the ways in which we spend our money. With such a wealth of good traditional and modern books for children, £1·50 may seem a high price to pay for this one.

*Joanna Matthews* Trumper is a fairly static character and many of the stories are Rospa-inspired adventures of the five-finger family, one of whom inevitably gets involved in an accident in each story. The moral of these stories may be worth presenting but I would find it boring to have to read them over often enough for the moral to sink in.

---

**Let's play maths** by Michael Holt and Zoltan Dienes (Penguin, 95p)

---

*Brenda Crowe* If everyone had fathers or uncles like this maths would be no problem! What child won't echo the advice: 'Never make a moral issue of a child's mistake . . .'? And which of us hasn't learned through experience that 'Parents can make too much of a "thing" of playing games'?

There are games to while away a car journey, games for picnics, games to play in the kitchen, games with clothes lines, card games and plenty more besides for assorted ages and stages. What's more, they really and truly *are* games, the authors leave you in no doubt of this – there is no hint of doing-your-child-good, no jargon about numeracy and number concepts, no pill under the sugar-coating. These men actually want us to play with our children, the sort of games that spring naturally to mind if you combine a mathematical mind with being a child-loving adult.

*Mollie Clarke* Strictly speaking, this book (for four to 11 year olds) is not in the age-range required for this exercise but the familiar philosophy emerges: the secret lies in catching him young enough before the mind 'hardens'. Experience shows that youngsters, if started young enough, can learn such seemingly way out things as logical reasoning, mathematical patterns and how words are put together. These are the ideas which are 'built into the structure' of the games.

The authors prepare parents for the exercise by giving a brief description of the new maths and the relationship between the mathematics and children's natural interests in sorting, matching and making connections between social, geographical, familial and linguistic connections.

Part two is a potted guide to child psychology which underlines possible pitfalls ahead. Only parents with lots of stamina will proceed beyond this point to part three which discusses the games themselves.

The idea behind this book is excellent. Mathematics is part of life and everyday learning and, above all, it is fun. The authors know what they are doing and why; they have a personal and professional understanding of children as well as of mathematics. The book itself is attractively designed with good spacing, irresistible titles and cartoon-like illustrations. It is the junior counterpart of mathematical puzzle books for adults.

And, like the adult books, it can produce a sense of failure and disappointment if the kind of help is not forthcoming, in the right way, at the right moment. The exercises seem to me to be deceptively simple and to demand a fairly high level of mathematical understanding, on the part of the adults involved. However, given this expertise and time for leisurely progression from set one to set 10, the book will prove immensely valuable.

*Joanna Matthews* The most specialist of all the books, this deals with a subject that still makes many adults wince. But the authors soon point out that the maths they are dealing with is not about number but about relationships, logic and the properties of things. Both entertaining and instructional, the 'games' they have devised would appeal to the bright four year old but would best be left to somewhat older children. Once the child has started school the present-day parent can feel at a loss about new maths, but this book would help to get children and parents back together on the same track.

# CHECKLIST OF PRE-SCHOOL MATERIALS FOR PARENTS

**Part one: early learning theory**

*How to raise a brighter child* by Joan Beck (Souvenir, £1·25, Fontana 45p)
*Reading and writing before school* by Felicity Hughes (Cape £1·25)
*Learning and playing* by Eileen Elias (Pitman £1·80)
*How to help a child at home* by Michael Newby and Kathleen Hartley (Home and School Council, 25p)
*The vital years and your child* by Audrey Bilski (Souvenir £2·20)

**Part two: pre-reading books**

*Home-start books* by Lesley Anne Ivory (Burke, hardback cloth 45p each; limp cloth 35p each)
*Bright-start books* by Althea (Souvenir, prices range between 50p and 60p)
*First steps in reading books* various authors (Benn, 50p each)
*Sparks books* various authors (Blackie, 12p each)
*Mother-and-child playbooks* (Young world productions, 15p each)
*Pictures and words books* by Elizabeth Goodacre (Blackie, 15p each)
*Book plus cassette* series (Holmes McDougall, £2·95 (£1·35 for book only)
*Storycards and picture map: a day in the country* by Sally Cedar (Cape, 95p)

**Part three: pre-school kits**

*Teach your baby to read* by Glenn Doman (Cape; kit £1·60, book £1·25)
*The parents' guidance kit for the under fives* by John Godwin (Cressrelles, £3·95)
*Training in basic cognitive skills* by Margaret Paull and Simon Haskell (ESA; 69p per pack of ten plus 50p for handbook)
*Training in motor skills* by Margaret Paull and Simon Haskell (ESA; 84p per pack of ten plus 50p for handbook)
*The three four five nursery course* by Iris Grender (Three four five Ltd, £11·75)

**Part four: practical activities**

*Learning with mother books 1–5* by E. and H. Wingfield (Ladybird, 18p each)
*Ladybird playbooks 1 and 2* by E. and H. Wingfield (Ladybird, 18p each)
*Day-by-day learning books* various authors (Hamlyn, 65p each)
*Help your child at home books* by John Akers (Caversham, various prices ranging from 12½p to 62½p)
*Busy books 1–6* (Collins, 58p for the six)
*You can draw the seaside* by Brian Paine (Cressrelles, 80p)
*Starting points series* edited by Harry Pluckrose (Evans, 45p each)
*You can make it books* prepared in consultation with Henry Pluckrose (Nelson, 25p each)
*Mother's help* edited by Susan Dickinson (Collins, £1·50; Fontana 50p)
*Not yet five* by Gwenda Bartram (ESA, 75p)
*Playing, learning and living* by Vera Roberts (Black, £1·25)
*Playgroup activities* by Brenda Crowe (Pre-school Playgroups Association, 50p plus 7p postage)
*Pre-school activities* by Dorothy and John Pickering (Batsford, £1·50)
*Pre-school play* by Kenneth Jameson and Pat Kidd (Studio Vista, £1·95)
*Trumper's playgroup book* by Delphine Evans (Blackie, £1·50)
*Let's play maths* by Michael Holt and Zoltan Dienes (Penguin, 50p)

## Stop press materials

This series of articles was originally published in WHERE during 1974 and 1975. So that we wouldn't miss out any useful materials that have appeared since then, we went back to our panel of three for their latest recommendations.

**Early learning theory**

*Your child's play* (Pan, 60p)
*Understanding the under-fives* by Donald Baker (Evans, £2·95)
*Understanding your baby* by Dorothy Baldwin (Ebury Press, £1·35)
*Problems of your child's vital years* by Audrey Bilski (Souvenir £3·50)
*Baby learning through baby play* by Dr Ira Gordon (Sidgwick and Jackson, £1·25)
*Child learning through child play* by Dr Ira Gordon, Barry Guinagh and Emile Jester (also £1·25)
*The continuum concept* by Jean Lerdloff (Duckworth, £3·95)
*State of play* edited by Roger Owen (BBC Publications, 75p)
*I've made a people* by Vera Roberts (A and C Black, £1·50)
*Focus on meaning* by Joan Tough (Allen and Unwin, £1·75)

**Pre-reading books**

*The Berenstain bear's new baby* by the Berenstains (Collins, 45p)
*Balooky Klujypod* by Cutler and Oxenbury (Heinemann, £1·90)
*When Violet died* by Mildred Kantrowitz (Bodley Head, £1·20)
*Harriet's naughty morning* by Jean Strachan (Transworld, 15p)

**Books on practical activities**

*First art* by Warren Farnworth (Evans, £2·50)
*Musical activities for young children* by Jean Gilbert (Ward Lock, £2·95)
*Towards reading* by Nonie Hunter (MacDonald Education, 95p)
*Play with a purpose for the under-sevens* by E. M. Matterson (Penguin, new edition, 75p)

# CHOOSING PRE-SCHOOL MATERIALS

**As a postscript to our series on pre-school materials for parents, we asked each of our three assessors to give a neat checklist of the points she felt parents should consider when on the point of choosing a book or kit for their children.**

**Joanna Matthews writes:**

You must choose for yourself and your children, but I like books that:

☐ look nice, feel nice and smell nice, because I don't go back to them if they don't

☐ are reassuring and make me feel that we are doing quite well as a family and not getting it all wrong

☐ are practical without being too directive, and are frank about what children can do without interference and when they need and benefit from adult help or support.

I'm suspicious of books that:

☐ have titles beginning 'How to . . .' – there aren't always right answers

☐ contain the idealised middle-class family complete with cat, dog and lawn-mower. These are designed for a preconceived market and the people aren't real

☐ use words like 'child management' and 'IQ' or make parents feel they must have 'successful' children.

---

**Brenda Crowe writes:**

*On early learning theory* The first essential is that you are honest with yourself. Ask yourself what sort of person and parent you are at this particular moment.

☐ Do you know yourself to be competitive and ambitious, both for yourself and your child? Then watch out that your desires for your child are not at odds with his temperament and abilities, and take care he doesn't begin to sense that he must be clever in order to be loved.

☐ Instead of seeking out books to project him forwards (particularly in one skill, such as reading), search for those that are concerned for all-round development.

☐ Do you know yourself to be lacking in confidence? If so, be careful not to assume that anybody who can write a book must be cleverer than you, and therefore to be believed and followed.

☐ Look for the books that are gentle in their approach, written by people you feel you would like if you met them.

☐ Stick to books that reinforce your 'good' feelings, and lead you on from there.

*On pre-reading books* The same advice still applies to this section, but extra awareness is needed. Do you enjoy books, particularly children's books? Do you enjoy sharing books with children?

If you can't (for one of many reasons) be physically or emotionally involved, still provide books of contrasted sizes and content, and create a friendly atmosphere with your child and the books on a rug on the floor or in an armchair near you, or seated at a low table, while you settle to do something that has to be done – ironing, painting, washing-up.

The choice of books you share in this way will be governed by the size and clarity of the picture from your particular distance. But go on offering other books, too, because slowly you may be able to help him to enjoy books alone and you may even find that you begin to enjoy them with him.

☐ If you love books you may have strong feelings about which are 'good' books and which are 'bad'. Let your child have a wide range so that slowly he can develop his own taste.

*On pre-school kits* First, ask yourself why you want a teaching kit? There are many parents who don't feel they could cope with books of a theoretical nature, but thankfully buy kits in the comforting knowledge that they will be told what to do. If you want to get-him-on, then the previous notes may suggest lines of thinking that you need to follow-up. But if you are sure that, without any sense of pressure, you just want to enjoy your child, and to offer him interests, pleasures and things-to-do as an optional extra, then still examine each kit both through your eyes and your child's.

☐ How do you react to fiddly things? Steer

From WHERE 103 (April 1975)

clear of anything that is going to irritate you in case your irritation communicates itself to your child. Steer clear also if you are particularly talented with your hands and are likely to be irritated by your child's present level of manual dexterity.

□ Ask yourself again and again 'Is this particular activity worth doing? What will we both get out of it? Is it just our pleasure in doing things together? If so, are there different things that we could do together which would be more natural, more satisfying and more aesthetically pleasing?'

*On practical activities* Yet again, know yourself, your child, and your motives.

□ The best books leave the child free to follow his own line of exploration, so that he learns-by-doing rather than by being told or being shown. These books will also explain that young children work from minute to minute without any end-product in view – this is real play, the play that is the teacher in itself.

□ Steer clear of books that require children to copy things. The copying stage comes all too quickly, and we need to encourage them to be sturdy individualists in their work and play (they won't know which is which if it is real play!).

□ Seek, too, books that will sharpen your own awareness of shapes, colours, textures, books that will help you to see as children see, with eyes full of wonder and curiosity.

---

**Mollie Clarke writes:**

On *learning theory,* look for:

*Authenticity* the propounder of the theories should be someone with up-to-date information about child development and relevant research in this field.

*Empathy* the writer should be able to relate his theories to first-hand practical experience in this dimension of education and/or parenthood.

*Relevance* the advice given should relate to the parent's and child's particular needs and also to the facilities available.

*Practical help* detailed programmes requiring expensive equipment and/or continuous interaction between parent and child are inappropriate for most parents.

*Flexibility* advice which sets up models of early learning with too closely defined standards and goals may produce anxiety and stress for the participators.

*Respect for childhood* any early learning project should take account of the need for genuine incentives, the development of play and the wide-ranging nature of a young child's hidden curriculum. The structures imposed by a 3R orientated syllabus may do more harm than good.

For *pre-reading books* look closely at:

*Content* early reading material should be easily understood and, for this reason, the content should – to a great extent – mirror the individual child's personal experience.

*Language* even short and uncomplicated language structures can set good (or bad) literary standards. The language of pre-reading books should reflect the response-range of the children concerned. It should never represent an adult's attempt to 'talk-down' to little children.

*Pictures* the illustrations and the text are interdependent; one should provide a clear clue to the other and any ambiguity will diminish the value of the exercise. It goes without saying (or does it?) that the illustrations should be of high quality.

*Style* all books at all levels can be interesting, stimulating, humorous or straight boring, and pre-reading books are no exception. If they fail to grasp the adult's attention they will almost certainly have the same effect on children.

*Method and medium* if the pre-reading book emphasises a particular method (or medium), check with the local school before starting on the programmes. Differing approaches may confuse the child.

On *pre-school kits* look closely at:

*Aims and objectives* kits vary from those which set out to teach children how to form letters of the alphabet to those which attempt to enhance the life-style of under-fives and their parents. Ask yourself if you want to achieve what a kit sets out to do?

*Alternatives* are there better (and cheaper) ways of developing a particular skill or aptitude?

*Suitability* is the material relevant for *your* child in *his* environment? Overseas kits republished in this country often leave much to be desired.

*Practicality* take a shrewd look at kits which (a) are based on small, highly destructible and difficult-to-manipulate cardboard pieces; (b) require expensive and not-easily obtainable supporting materials; (c) do not provide opportunities for the child to work on his own. Too much dependence on the adult is a poor start to education.

*Commitment for parents and children* the designers of some kits make it quite clear that they consider the syllabus and the daily routine sacrosanct. No issues should be dodged! You must therefore decide if you are capable of fitting all this into your daily lives and if, in fact, the results will be worth the effort.

*Interest-value* unless the material provides the right kind of incentive, you'll have to work hard to maintain the child's interest.

On *practical activities* look closely at:

*The end results* are the end results (as defined by text and illustration) aesthetically pleasing or artily and craftily vulgar?

*The designer's objectives* are children being led to develop their own spontaneous interests and skills or are the suggestions directed towards the reproduction of prescribed models? Exercises of the second kind are likely to inhibit future creativity.

*Techniques* are these so much above or below the children's capacity that they cannot fail to feel frustrated? Are they perhaps so complicated that you the parents have constantly to be consulted? Or are they, perhaps, a little beyond your capabilities too? Somewhere, between the pages, should be a guarantee of success.

*Incentives* are the objects of the exercise sufficiently well related to children's play interests? For example, most children are not urgently motivated to make a night-light holder!

*The quality of instruction* is the text written in words that children will understand and are the illustrations clear and unambiguous? Does the production (format, illustration and the glimpse of pleasures-in-store) excite children?

# RECYCLING FOR PRE-SCHOOL MUMS

Edna Golding

RECYCLING IS A new word, but an old process. My mother and grandmother called it 'waste not, want not' when they had to organise play for their young children.

Today, with technological development on one hand, and wastage on the other, we have even more objects and materials that can be recycled, for the benefit of our own young children. It also conserves materials, and provides 'something for nothing'.

Recycling is discovery, and once the family has grasped the idea, there are endless possibilities. It can provide the young child with imaginative and creative play, art experiences, opportunities for physical development, and even pre-maths and science experience! I have listed below some commonplace objects and how they can be transformed for your pre-school child. Always ensure though that whatever you use is hygienic, does not constitute a danger to health, and is safe (*eg* no jagged edges, lead-free). I will leave you to experience the excitement of further discoveries.

## Household containers

**Cardboard boxes** This is how you enter the game, for cardboard boxes are the first priority. Collect strong boxes of various sizes, several of each size. Shopping expeditions at the local supermarket are the most obvious hunting ground. The appearance of these boxes can be enhanced by a coat of emulsion paint. Usually carefully hoarded emulsion paint has turned to an iron-stained solid lump by the time one wants to use it, so why not use it to create an easy way to identify contents by colour and to hide brand names?

These boxes become the storage containers for recycling discoveries. Extra boxes are always good to store trainsets, construction toys, model cars and so on, which never seem to be replaceable in the boxes in which they were first packed unless you have endless time and the mind of a genius.

**Tins** If you use a rotary can opener (to make sure that there are no rough edges), tins, washed and painted, can be used for storage.

Join them together in clusters with blobs of 'metal-to-metal' compounds. Glues *won't* work!

Different-sized tins can be made to fit inside each other, or used in tower building.

Punch holes in the base of the tin. Several tins with a different number of holes, can make bathtime fun.

**Plastic** Add to the container collection by halving the gallon or half-gallon plastic bottle. Lego and conkers need no longer litter the floor!

**Egg boxes** The readymade partitions in egg boxes show off collections to great advantage. They are easily stored when your child is no longer actively interested in the collection but is not sure whether he 'won't need it next week, and it's not rubbish!'

Egg boxes make wonderful sorting boxes if used in conjunction with the button box (see *Buttons*). Mixed powder paint can be kept in the polystyrene boxes as the lids help to stop evaporation between usage.

## Clothing and materials

**Buttons** Button-holes cut out of garments with enough surrounding material to be able to mount the two parts on an old jumble sale picture frame. (Laces, zips, hooks and eyes, press studs, can be used in the same way.) Children can learn the intricacies of clothing in an unhurried play-

*Here are more elaborate examples of what you can make from junk . . .*

Drawings from *Models from Junk* by Brenda B. Jackson

From WHERE 106 (July 1975)

way, instead of discovering the complexities when time waits for no man – or child.

**Life-sized doll** Sew thick tights at the waist onto a polo-necked, long sleeved jumper. Then sew mittens onto the end of the jumper's sleeves. Use a balaclava to form the head. Stuff the 'body' with a safe filling (*eg* old tights) through the face piece of the balaclava. Lastly, sew in a face piece and paint on a happy face. Result? One life-sized doll to hug or hate as the mood dictates.

**Texture matching** Cut two small squares from different textured material so that children can play 'feeling games' and match-up pairs.

**Picture making** Cut material into prefabricated shapes: round, square, circles, roof shapes, and so on. Children can use them, along with paste and cardboard, to produce collage or representational pictures depending upon their stage of development.

## Heavyweights

**Magnets** Old tv sets contain large circular magnets which are a constant source of pleasure and delight for children of all ages.

**Prams** The curved body of the larger size prams (*eg* Osmath) makes an efficient rocking boat. The wheels can become a means of transport, if you cover the frame with an offcut of blockboard and fix with conduit pipe fitting clips.

**Old curtains** Pull the rufflet tape strings as tight as possible to make a ruff collar. Sew a piece of tape, or ribbon, to each side of ruff so that the original curtain can now be worn as a cloak. The colour, type and quality of the curtain will dictate the imaginative play of the wearer *eg* net curtaining for brides, velvet for the ball.

**Car parts** Depending upon the size and space available, *tyres* for outside use add much to the extension of imaginative play. Prop them up against boxes to make a lorry. They can be suspended in a mini-assault course and a large tractor tyre can make the actual surround to a sandpit. A coat of car upholstery paint not only transforms the tyres but protects and stops any black tyre marks.

A tyre with the centre filled with tough plywood, fitted with four disused castors, two rope handles or towing rope attached, makes a very versatile piece of outdoor play equipment.

An old *steering wheel,* still in its column, can be set into a concrete base, using a small cardboard box as a mould. Hey presto, the means of driving an imaginary lorry, bus, car or boat. This wheel will outlive dozens of the plastic variety; it can be left out in the garden without worry. So far I can tell of nine years' usage!

**Outgrown playpens** The wooden variety can convert into a collapsible den. Cover with old jumble sale curtaining (make allowances for the folding). Remove two of the upright bars from one side and you have a 'den' for in or outdoor play.

## Kitchen finds

**Bun tins and buns** Don't throw away old bun tins. These tins make very good moulds in which to set melted down crayon stubs. Young children appreciate the large size of the crayon, and older

children seize upon them with glee for bark rubbing and so on.

Should you ever have a disaster when baking cakes, decide whether the item, if continued to be slowly baked and then varnished, will provide goodies for the proverbial dolls' tea party.

**Plastic washing-up liquid containers** These can be cut in half, the top inverted into the base, so making a safe paint pot. The dripping paint will run back down the funnel shape that has been created.

Containers left whole, but painted or covered in surplus wall paper, can be converted into basic musical instruments when filled with such household items as rice, dried peas, pearl barley and so on.

**Onion skins** Use these for dyeing. Tie and dye old vests by boiling for half an hour in onion water. To make the pattern, bind round pebbles with thick string. The result? Yellow t-shirts.

**Disused bread trays** These trays can be converted into tables, or display boards mounted above the bed. Better still, they are shallow enough to be mounted on castors at reinforced corners, and with a rope handle attached, fit under a bed.

**Plastic sacks** Fertilizer sacks and similar sacks from well-known chain-stores provide the material for aprons. Cut out a simple bottle shape with pinking scissors, make a hole for the head somewhere beneath the 'neck' of the bottle. Staple ties on to the side from the off-cuts.

From these examples, you can soon begin to see objects and materials for use other than their original intention. Small items that can be used in a recycling fashion, are: aluminium foil, books, brushes, buttons, bottle tops, coat hangers, combs, cellophane, cardboard, crayons, conkers, cocktail sticks, coloured paper, Christmas cards, doilies, dinky car wheels, elastic, egg boxes, fur, feathers, foam rubber, felt, fertilizer bags, fir cones, grasses, handbags, jars, jewellery, jelly moulds, jumpers, jute, knitting needles, kitchen utensils, kegs, keys, knobs, lamp-shades, lolly-sticks, latches, leaves, lino, lenses, links, magazines, matchboxes, milk-bottle tops, netting, newspapers, nails, overalls, odd socks, paper cups, pails, paper clips, pebbles, polystyrene trays, ribbon, records, rubber bands, shells, sequins, straw, spectacle frames, tiles, thread, tape, tissue paper, wool, wood, wire, wallpaper, yoghurt cartons.

*Edna Golding is a lecturer at the Rachel McMillan college of education in Deptford.*

**bookbox**

*How to recycle your rubbish* by J. Allen and S. Finmark (Studio Vista, £1·50)
*Junk on the move* and *Models from junk* by Brenda B. Jackson (Evans, 30p and 35p respectively)
*The musical instrument recipe book* shows how to make musical instruments from simple, everyday materials (Penguin education, 50p)
*Playgroup activities* (60p from the Pre-school Playgroups Association, Alford House, Aveline Street, London SE11).

# THE LIFE OF A TOY

## Betty Jerman

**Children respond to toys in their own way – and are about as likely to go for toys marked for 'four to six year olds' when they're in that age group, and those alone, as they are to wear only vests or trousers marked in that way. Every child will defy at least one of the age limits for toys suggested in this report. But we hope that none the less these limits will be right for a child far more often than they are wrong, and will prove useful to parents not only in terms of picking possible toys for each age, but also for seeing which toys are the stayers – the ones which, if they take with children at all, will be played with for years and years.**

I SHOULD SAY very firmly at the outset that you cannot cost a toy in terms of so many pounds for so many years' play. The development of children is too complicated for that. At times children will go through considerable changes over a comparatively short period, for example, from birth to two years. At other times they will make slower changes over longer periods. Both will affect how long a toy has appeal for a child. And then there is the unknown quantity of an individual child's personality and interests.

The sheer variety of what comes under the generic term of 'toys' also defeats any attempt to put a precise term on the life span of many of them. After all adults make jigsaws, planes from plastic kits and large-scale models from Lego without the excuse of playing with children. And they may cherish a teddy or a miniature roundabout which they first got at two years old.

For all these reasons many toymakers are wary about marking containers with age limits, other than those including small swallowable items or elements requiring some maturity to handle. There are too many variables. But I make the attempt here in order to give some basis for choice for those who feel slightly bewildered by the range and variety of toys now available.

Toys fall roughly into two categories. The first stimulates the child's physical, emotional and intellectual development. One toy may fit quite a brief stage. The rattle is the most easily recognisable example. It provides sound, texture and shape at a specific growth stage. No one could complain because a normal three year old was not still playing with his rattle, but it seems harder to recognise that a jigsaw with a few large pieces also fits a comparable short period and yet is just right for that stage.

The second category of toys offers experience. Small scale gardening tools may

*continued on p67*

## How long do toys last and what age children do they appeal to?

**Toys lasting up to a year**

mobile *one month to a year*
teething rings *six months to a year*
bell cubes or blocks *six months to a year*
push and pull toys *one year to two years*
jigsaw (25 pieces) *three years to four years*
plastic modelling kits, first and second series (1/72 scale) *seven years to eight years*
plastic modelling kits, third series (1/72 scale) *nine years to ten years*

**Toys lasting up to 18 months**

suspended cradle toy *three months to 18 months*
rattles *four months to 18 months*
pram beads *four months to 18 months*
foam bricks *six months to two years*
baby shapes *six months to two years*
grippable ball *six months to two years*
wooden doll *nine months to two years*
unbreakable mirror *nine months to two years*
miniature wooden roundabout *18 months to three years*
screwing toys *18 months to three years*
hammer pegs *18 months to three years*
posting box *18 months to three years*
low riding or rocking toys *18 months to three years*
lift-up jigsaw puzzles *18 months to three years*
large plastic fitting bricks *two and a half years to four years*

**Toys lasting up to two years**

peg or ball tunnel *nine months to two and a half years*
baby walker *one year to three years*
teddy bear *one year to three years*

hobby horse *three years to five years*
wooden take-apart vehicles *three years to five years*
jigsaw (50 pieces) *four years to six years*
nurse and doctor kits *four years to six years*

**Toys lasting up to three years**

foam ball *six months to three years*
nesting blocks or beakers *nine months to three years*
graded threading rings *18 months to four years*
abacus *18 months to four years*
small wooden vehicles *18 months to four years*
wooden train *18 months to four years*
doll's pram *two years to five years*
modelling materials *two years to five years*
jigsaw (12 pieces) *two and a half years to five years*
plastic or wooden train set *three years to six years*
finger or glove puppets *three years to six years*
farm machinery *four years to seven years*
sewing machine *seven years to ten years*

**Toys lasting up to four years**

washable plastic soft toys *nine months to four years*
rag doll *one year to five years*

From WHERE 94 (July 1974)

wooden animals *18 months to five years*
telephone *two years to six years*
baby doll *two years to six years*
puzzle clock *two and a half years to six years*
big crayons *two and a half years to six years*
wooden constructional sets *three years to seven years*
picture games (dominoes, snap, lotto) *three years to seven years*
large metal loading trucks *three years to seven years*
varied stuffed soft toys *three years to seven years*
doll's tea set *three years to seven years*
cookery set *three years to seven years*
broom and household equipment *three years to seven years*
musical instruments (tambourine, drum) *three years to seven years*
shop equipment (cash register) *four years to eight years*
weighing scales *four years to eight years*
giant magnet *four years to eight years*
traditional dominoes and draughts *six years to ten years*
childsize carpentry tools *six years to ten years*
childsize gardening tools *six years to ten years*
teenage doll *seven years to 11 years*
Action man *seven years to 11 years*
toy theatre *eight years to 12 years*
conjuring set *eight years to 12 years*
chemistry set *ten years to 14 years*
electronic kit *ten years to 14 years*
plastic model kits /(1/24 scale and above) *11 years to 15 years*
crafts, candle making, lino printing, latex moulding, enamelling and so on *11 years to 15 years*

**Toys lasting up to five years**
bath toys *nine months to five years*
Tomte vinyl vehicles *nine months to five years*
child's musical box *18 months to six years*
small diecast vehicles *18 months to six years*
solid legless dolls, plus accessories *two and a half years to seven years*
wheelbarrow *three years to eight years*
easel/blackboard *three years to eight years*
farm and 200 animals *three years to eight years*
Wendy house or shop *three years to eight years*
larger diecast vehicles *five years to ten years*
traditional dolls' house and furniture *five years to ten years*
Meccano *seven years to 12 years*
modelling clay *seven years to 12 years*
kite *seven years to 12 years*
Fischertechnik 200 *seven years to 12 years*

**Toys lasting up to six years**
doll's cot *two years to eight years*
paints (poster/powder) and big brushes *two and a half years to eight years*
wooden blocks *three years to nine years*
garage *three years to nine years*
Construct-o-straws *four years to ten years*
nice dressable doll (for example, Sasha) *six years to 12 years*
metal puzzles *six years to 12 years*

be the foundation of a life-time's love; a toy theatre the foundation of a life-time's interest in drama. There are many other examples, the most obvious being the chemistry set, frequently given in the hope of getting a budding scientist. The child may still turn to golf or pop. The seed was still worth sowing.

So in reading this guide to the life span of toys, take it that some toys are open-ended, that some children will use toys sooner or later than others, and that this is a guide to the average ages within which a toy should get maximum use. The list starts with the toys with the shortest life and moves on to those with a progressively longer play appeal. Within each category toys for the youngest children are listed first.

board games with tactical skill *eight years to 14 years*
powered models, motor racing, trains, planes *nine years to 15 years*

**Toys lasting up to seven years**
flower press *five years to 12 years*
mini microscope *seven years to 14 years*

**Toys lasting up to eight years**
outdoor slide or swing *two and a half years to ten years*
junior goal *six years to 14 years*

**Toys lasting up to nine years**
sandpit and tools *18 months to ten years*
climbing frame *three years to 12 years*

**Toys lasting up to ten years**
Lego *four years to 14 years*

# 5 Profile Hillfields Nursery Centre

# PROFILE
# HILLFIELDS NURSERY CENTRE, COVENTRY

## Anne Garvey

HILLFIELDS IS A big place, an estate built on part of bombed-out Coventry. Its scale is massive. High-rise flats rise and rise. Roads intersect on stilts, meet and form and bridge each other. There are underpasses and flyovers and tiled murky subways. Underneath the ring road that skirts the city, children were playing in a gravelly area of swings and fountains and roundabouts. Above their heads the traffic was roaring and fuming its way towards the motorway.

The nursery is in the middle of Hillfields. Stepping inside it is a big move. I felt rather like Gulliver, shifting from the land of the giants to the tiny world of the Lilliputians. Outside everything is massy and dizzily spacious as if built for a race of fifteen footers. Inside it is all scaled down. Suddenly the furniture is miniature, the equipment is knee-high.

The children find it quite a switch too. 'Some of them are just totally bewildered for the first week,' the headmistress Mrs Johnson told me. 'If you live 15 floors up, there's lots of skills you miss out on. For instance most of them simply cannot negotiate a step when they come here, so we have sort of huge building bricks to practise on.' When you think of it how can they possibly learn at home? They never have the opportunity to climb? They just stand in a lift and it hurtles them up to their flat.

Size and scale are very important. The children have a strange sort of life. Although it's all huge around here, they are mostly confined to tiny cells of rooms. I know there are play areas but could you really let a child under five play so far away from you? It would be ridiculously dangerous.

Hillfields nursery is low and odd-shaped – a one-storey building with lots of floor-length windows and glass doors. It was a beautiful day and the children were processing in and out of the small courtyard, wheeling prams, dragging toys, harnessed to each other or on their own, squealing and squeaking and giggling and fratching.

The rooms were open plan but cluttered with an impossible amount of toys and bricks and sand pits and wendy houses. 'We want them to have the experience of something other than four corners and four walls,' said the headmistress. 'And we have an orchard here as well. Would you believe it in the middle of all this concrete? It must be almost a physical relief to see greenery after brick and glass for years.'

Mrs Johnson has a strong, open sympathy with the home environment of the children in the nursery.

Of course it's not just the physical side that matters, but I do think it plays an enormous part. Mothers feel trapped up there. No wonder so many of them are down at the doctor's demanding 'pick-me-ups': this area is awash with anti-depressants. We cannot just say 'we are a nursery: this is education'. We must deal with the community. And these cursed flats are part of the community.

You know I sometimes hear mothers telling me that they'll try and catch for another baby – so they can get out of the high rise, so that they'll get re-housed. It makes you quite frightened for the family. They are only just feeling their way through with the children they've already got. I usually tell them about other families I've known who have tried the same trick – and are still living in the same flat.

It's sad isn't it when your only escape hatch is another child.

The Hillfields nursery project is ambitious. But it's also sensible. It aims at making a united assault on the evils that restrict and inhibit and stunt a child's development. It wants to incorporate education and welfare and medicine. If a child is being ill-fed or is living in an emotionally pressured environment, then the nursery channels the facts to the welfare, to the social service agencies or to the doctor. Co-operation is the watchword.

Mrs Johnson pointed out that this hadn't been done in the past. There had been too many departmental rivalries – too much of the letter and none of the spirit of the law. When some of the families got into difficulties, they were visited by no fewer

*Pages 68/69:* Bob Bray

From WHERE 95 (August 1974)

than 12 different agencies. They all meant well. There was the education welfare officer and the ordinary social worker and the teacher from school and the officer from social security and the representative from the social services and the doctor. Hardly ever did the information come and go from the person who knew the child best outside his home, the class teacher.

Here we have groups of children who are cared for by specially-trained staff. They know what to look for and can usually spot any disturbance in the home. They tell me and I can get straight on to the social services – or the police. It might sound a bit slow even so, but if you knew the old system the way you have to work the cranking stiff machinery just to deliver a child from a dangerous home or to make sure that a distressed mother gets some help . . .

The nursery is geared to the long working day. It opens at 7 am and goes right through the day until six in the evening. Mrs Johnson sees this as essential if the nursery is really to be a service for the children who need it most – one-parent children or children with especially stressful backgrounds. Sometimes she takes them in quickly, after a crisis in the home; at other times she has to make them wait a little longer, until she has the space. Then she tries to give the children the extra compensatory boost that they need just before going to school.

When they eventually get to 'big school' they are so much better equipped. They can put their own clothes and shoes on and hold a pencil. They can choose. It's amazing the amount of children we get here who are totally bewildered by choice. They have to be coaxed into the process of making a decision. When they first see lots of alternatives they freeze, or become destructive. Gradually we can teach them to behave coolly, to consider options – even if it is only choosing from a tray of different coloured paints.

We walked around the nursery, picking our way through the comings and goings of the children. An impromptu little group squatted down on a bright red blanket and listened to a story. Other little figures tottered and toddled and lurched baby-like about, clutching knitted teddy bears and pushing prams. A four-year-old girl was ensnaring a tiny two year old in a hula hoop. 'Be careful with him, Chris,' warned one of the staff, 'he's only a very little boy'. The operation was gently superintended, not stopped.

Mrs Johnson recognises that it would be much easier if they were all segregated, but she really wants a family atmosphere – and so is prepared to risk all the potential clashes of different ages and stages.

Obviously there has to be some sort of sectioning off. Here we have babies of six weeks who need to be nursed and cuddled and left to sleep. And then there are the under twos who need to rest in the afternoons. They have to have a quiet place. We all want there to be some sort of rhythm to the children's lives. The day is a long one if they are left for the full time. There need to be times for singing and shouting and letting off steam, and times for keeping still. When the little ones wake up, they get a slice of apple and some milk – and they are raring to go again.

With so many children organisation is vital, a hidden sort of organisation. Mrs Johnson says she would hate the place to be regimented. But each child has a person they go to if they fall down and hurt themselves or when they want a quiet talk and someone's arm round them. When they first come she tries to give almost exclusive attention to them but as they get to know the nursery, she lets the staff/child ratio slacken off from one to four to one to 12. 'But of course the babies need more staff than anyone.'

**Kaleidoscope**

Visually Hillfields is magnificent. The children move about in a wonderland of colour and shape. Mobiles are hanging from the roof – we make our way about by dodging great cardboard birds suspended on long strings.

This week the theme is flying. That's what these things are, flapping in your face. Some of them are supposed to be aeroplanes.

She has a colour every week as well. When I was there it was black, and there was a corner draped in black velvet and witches' hats. Her idea is to allow the children to concentrate on one concept at a time.

The floor space has been ingeniously arranged. Hillfields has over a hundred children a day, but they all seem to be doing something different. There are private little spaces sectioned off into peaceful seclusion, there's a miniature house and next to it an art area with tiny seats and chairs. Another part of the open-plan floor houses the mobile objects, large cycles and moveable dogs on wheels.

We have to keep activities separate, otherwise the boisterous bike-riders are crashing into the quiet painters. The children have moods, sometimes they feel like letting rip, sometimes they want to make something of their own. We want the building to adapt to them and not the other way round.

Hillfields shows them the outside world as well, believing that they need to see there is something beyond the four walls of their own flat, bigger than the nursery can show them.

We are going to take the children to an airport – they aren't too young. After all they hear the jets screaming over all day. Even four year olds are entitled to know what their environment is all about. They have to live in it. This is the age when you can fire their imagination. This is why we are here: we aren't just baby-minders.

Round the entrance hall was a cluster of large pictures. One was a confusion of red and green and blue circles, squares and triangles all stuck firmly to red card – it was labelled 'A funny man with one leg'. Another was a chalk drawing on dark paper called simply, and boldly 'Trisha's picture'.

Mrs Johnson explained that the labels were really for the parents. When they saw some of the things their children did, they were quite amazed. You could see their attitude change over the year. When they first brought the children they weren't very interested in what the children were doing during the day. Most of them had been at work and they were just too exhausted to chat.

But they became intrigued and began looking about the place and the conversation changed gradually.

It's very gratifying to hear parents actually asking their children what's been going on here during the day.

In the garden two young men were bouncing children about with exhausting persistence. Helpers at the nursery, they are community service volunteers taking a year off before university. 'It's good for kids to have men about. They can roll around with them and jump on their stomachs and do all the things they can't do so easily with women staff.'

Lots of the Hillfields children hardly ever see their fathers – if there is one about. Many of them work late and sometimes the pressure of the small flats that they live in drives them down to the pub for the evening. The mothers are alone all day and then alone all night. 'The boys who help here are good for us and for the children. They help give the place balance.'

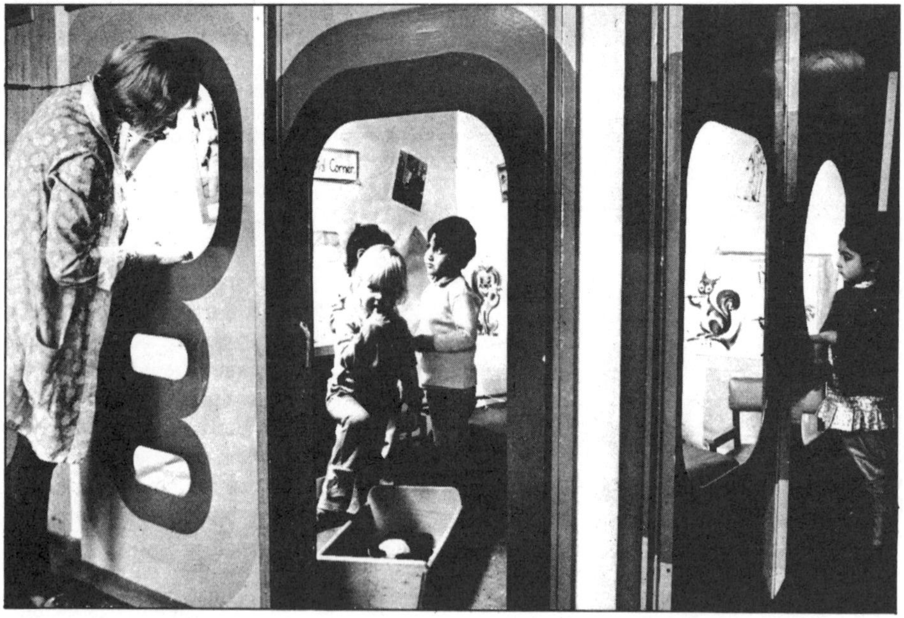

**Shifting and sifting**

The nursery at Hillfields exists in a highly volatile community. It serves a society that is constantly altering its nature. The staff know they must shift and adapt to the changing scene.

They cope with problems as they arise. And they crop up fast and furiously.

Their latest worry is the Asian mothers. They used to be the most stable and reliable of all the families. They were difficult to change but the nursery saw that as part of their virtue. The children were secure and the mothers always at home.

People used to worry about them not speaking English and all that sort of thing. But what is happening now is much more serious in my view. They have quite suddenly started going out to work. I don't know exactly what it is that drives them to these factories (they usually choose jobs where there is little exposure to spoken English – industrial assembly, that sort of thing). I suspect that it's mortgage payments that mostly force them out to work. Repayments have become crippling.

Many Asians do gravitate towards private housing rather than go into corporation or privately rented accommodation. But whatever the reason, the nursery is getting the backlash. Mothers come to Mrs Johnson with tiny babies and say 'You look after him?' She has to tell them no. She has so many more needy cases – single mothers who simply have to work, young schoolgirls with babies who actually have to be in class during the day. Or children with only a working father to care for them. She says that she cannot accept children on the basis that their mother wants a job, even if she needs it very badly.

**In the right place?**

The tremendous waiting list at Hillfields is an alarming fact that stares the administration in the face every day. The file of hopeful applicants is thick. And yet while the mothers work, the children are left *somewhere* – it is an indisputable unpalatable fact. Some of them are farmed out to registered childminders, more are sent to unregistered, illegally-functioning minders. Some are even left on their own.

'You can tell the ones who have been with unsuitable people,' says the head, 'they are as plain to us as that door post. These are the frightened children inhibited with each other, apprehensive of adults. The educational setbacks they suffer are incalculable.'

Often they are left all day just sitting on a sofa or lying in a cot. There is no stimulation, no entertainment, no constructive play, in fact there is very little play at all. It's messy and many of the minders just do not want mess, their houses are too small to accommodate little children for long working days.

Hillfields wants parents to see what wonderful things their children can do. It wants them to develop as much as they can, it feels the need to teach the families and the children together, to educate child and parent.

As I left two little four year olds sped past us on bicycles, a group of smaller children splashed each other with water. In a quiet corner the very young afternoon sleepers were being gently woken and given their snack.

That is what breaks your heart, the ones that aren't here.

# FACT-BOX ON HILLFIELDS

## Who runs it

A multidisciplinary project set up in 1971 by the Coventry education department and the public health department.

The centre has a management committee made up of city councillors, representatives of the social services and education departments, and local residents. The local residents are elected by parents with children at the centre, but parents don't work at the centre.

## Who pays what

Initially funded by a £65,000 urban aid grant. Now wholly financed by the local authority.

A parents' association runs some fund-raising events, but it is primarily concerned with organising social activities for parents who cannot get out and about very much.

Attendance fees vary according to time spent at the centre and family circumstances. If a child attends from nine till four the usual charge is 35p a day which includes a meal at lunchtime. Longer periods which include having a second meal either in the morning or the early evening would cost 65p a day. Low income families are charged on a reduced scale. Overall the fees are lower than for other day nurseries run by the social services department. There is no charge if a child is absent, and there is no holding fee.

## Who goes there

There are 100 places available for children between six weeks and five years old. Places for children under two are limited to a couple of dozen. At the moment about 70 children attend full-time with 60 children going part-time for 2½ hours in the morning or the afternoon.

There is a large turnover because of children going on to primary school and because the local population is fairly mobile. Since opening in 1971, the centre has catered for about 1,000 children in all.

## Who works there

The staff of 20 includes the head and deputy head, two assistant teachers, a senior nursery nurse, a group of nursery nurses and an orderly.

The head of the centre, Mrs Margaret Johnson, is an ex-primary school headmistress. She is leaving this year and a new head will be appointed in September 1976.

## How it works

The centre is open from 7 am till 6 pm, Monday to Friday, 49 weeks of the year. It is closed for Coventry's industrial holiday fortnight in July and for one week at Christmas.

The staff work staggered hours and have staggered holidays. Most are there at some time during each day, unless on leave. About a quarter of the children start at 7 am. The majority of the children attend from 9 till 4. About 20 to 25 are there until 6 in the evening.

Parents who want their children to attend go on to a waiting list. The list currently has 300 names.

When the centre was set up an advisory group pinpointed those children who should get priority:

- ☐ children from one-parent families
- ☐ children whose mothers work through necessity
- ☐ children from low income families
- ☐ handicapped children
- ☐ immigrant children
- ☐ children living in high-rise flats
- ☐ children of mothers under psychiatric care
- ☐ children of parents who jointly run a business

Mrs Johnson has since added a further category for children whose parents both work and the mother does work of a recognised social need such as hospital work, teaching and so on.

Some children are recommended to the centre by welfare officers. Urgent cases can be given a place immediately.

# 6 Starting school

Kate Grillet

# STARTING SCHOOL: THE PROBLEMS CHILDREN FACE

Christopher Jarman

THE DAYS WHEN little children were dragged unwillingly to their first day at school, kicking and screaming with mum threatening 'Shut up or the teacher'll let you 'ave it' are largely over.

Most infant reception classes are such colourful, relaxed and friendly places that it is easy for an adult to underestimate the overwhelming impact that such a new experience may have for a child. The fact that there are toys and games, dressing-up clothes, guinea pigs or sand trays may make it seem like a child's paradise to the parent.

Unfortunately for the five year old, it often seems quite the opposite at first. Although the anxiety produced by this new experience is usually quickly overcome, it is a genuine anxiety. A little forethought by parents can do a great deal to relieve the situation.

**Danger zones**

The playground and the toilets are probably the areas which cause the most concern. In both these places the new child feels alone and without the support of adults. The playground is full of apparently enormous children all rushing around at full speed. Don't forget that although they all look like infants to us, six and seven year olds are 'the big ones' to a five year old. Just squat down at the school gate to a five year old's eye-level as you go into a school, and you will see the point. A sensitive infant teacher will often allow the little ones to stay in the classroom for a day or two during playtimes, and mothers can help by not leaving new children early at school for the first week, so that they have to face half an hour of perhaps a hundred strangers rushing around them in a vast playground. A child can cope with this after a week or two quite happily, when he has made a few friends and understands that his own classroom is quite a safe haven.

If your child is unhappy for the first day or two and cries or clings, do remember that the teacher, unless she is absolutely new, is very experienced in dealing with other people's children. The best thing is to leave your child with the teacher or headteacher and go. Out of sight out of mind is not a flattering thought for a parent, but except for a few cases of particularly nervous children, this is true.

A good deal can be done to ease entry into the infants school beforehand. Attending a playgroup or nursery school, part-time to begin with, is probably the best experience. Infant teachers constantly say to me that they can tell immediately those children who have been to playgroup or nursery school. They are usually socially more mature and settle in very quickly. This is a bigger blessing to the school than a child being able to read.

**Being a social being**

As a new parent, with an oldest child going to school for the first time, it is easy to overlook the most important aspects of this experience. So often the idea of school summons up the prospect of books, sums, reading, counting and so on. Some mothers worry in case their Sarah or Mark will be behind the others. So many problems would be solved if parents could understand the teachers' point of view, namely that academic performance in the three Rs is important, but *certainly not in those first few weeks at school.*

The most important factors so far as the teacher is concerned at this stage are largely social and emotional ones. This is because if at the very beginning the child is happy and can cope with the sheer mechanics of living in a large building, with perhaps two hundred other children and maybe ten strange new adults during the day, then all will be well later when the intellectual skills begin to be tackled. It is far more important that Sarah can recognise her own wellington boots among thirty other identical pairs than that she can add two and two for the moment. Parents need to use some imagination, particularly with clothing. No-one in that class is going to get a story read to them, let alone be taught a single word, if the teacher has to unbutton twenty pairs of trousers for the boys to go to the toilets and then button them up again.

Simple social training for your child in buttoning and unbuttoning his clothes, and either tying his own shoelaces or putting on slip-on shoes, is important. Try tying up eighty shoelaces for a class of five year olds and see how long it takes!

Again, if a child has never had a meal outside his own home, never eaten in a cafe or restaurant, then school dinner is probably


*Pages 74/75*: Richard Dykes
From WHERE 108 (September 1975)

going to be a very strange experience without his parents there. Many children have a private language about food as well as about the lavatory. A sensitive teacher pressed by 35 or 40 different new children all with their own private family languages will do her best to respond kindly but she is only human. Parents can really help their children by giving them some pre-school experiences of eating out and the socially accepted words for most human activities.

Parents should not be reticent about problems which may seem rather trivial or embarrassing to them. If a child is incontinent occasionally, do tell the teacher and leave an extra pair of pants with her. She won't mind at all; she will be grateful for your thoughtfulness. If he does not eat greens or fish or baked beans, then tell the teacher. It can save a lot of misunderstanding.

Don't send your infant to school with braces which he cannot undo himself or garments which unbutton down the back. Often a new school means new clothes and some unfamiliar fastenings for the child. He has enough that is new to cope with during that first week. At least let him or her wear shoes and trousers or dresses and coats that can be coped with from familiarity.

Pre-school visits and discussions with mothers are arranged in some schools. In two or three villages in my local area mothers are invited into school for group discussions during several afternoons with the headmistress, the infant teacher and the primary school adviser. In a circle with a cup of tea, an informal discussion in an easy atmosphere brings up most of the points that need to be discussed. These mothers are invited when their children are about three years old; that is two years before they are due to start. The skills and habits which would be most useful for the children to acquire are discussed. Pre-reading activities, suitable story books, suitable toys and pre-number games are talked about and a great deal of confidence is built up between mothers, children and the teachers long before that first school day.

**Reading**

I've already touched upon children's speech and vocabulary. They are a most important part of their social competence. A child's ability to start reading depends to a large extent upon his language development. His ability to cope with clothing, doors, washing himself, going to the lavatory, shoes is also dependent to a degree on his language and vocabulary. Some children start school hardly able to speak at all at five years old. Others may chatter away non-stop but in an entirely private family language. They then become unhappy and frustrated when neither the teacher nor the other children know what they are trying to say. This problem soon passes and children quickly pick up the classroom and the playground language.

An important point concerns the emotive question of reading. While it is quite possible to teach some children to read before they go to school, my own investigations with about 150 parents who had done this (*Children who read before going to school* in WHERE 57) showed that while it is seldom a disadvantage to a child, learning to read before school is not necessarily an advantage either. Should a parent be determined to do this, the best plan is to discuss it with the prospective school, and in particular the infant teacher into whose class the child is going, and take her advice. The advice of almost all the 150 parents in the survey was: 'If the child is not happy learning to read with mother, then stop it at once.' I have known a case where the anxiety for a child to read early had communicated itself from mother to child, resulting in an emotional conflict. This prevented the child from learning to read for several years.

A simple rule for games involving letter recognition, or for a child writing or knowing his own name is to use small letters at all times and *not capitals*. Capital letters are rarely seen in books except at the beginning of sentences. And teachers will want the children to know the lower case letters first.

Finally, remember that what you as a parent *feel* about school will communicate itself to your child regardless of what you *say* about it. So go along early to the school, meet the head and the staff, develop a positive, tolerant and enquiring attitude at first, and do give the teachers the benefit of the doubt. A single woman who has taught for five or ten years may not know your child as well as you do, but she will know more than many mothers about other people's children, and how yours will compare with them.

Starting school is a big day in children's lives. It holds far more significance to them than we realise. I am sure many people reading this can remember their first hour at school, let alone their first day, and most of us remember our first teacher. The incidents which loom largest in the memory belong very often to cloakrooms, corridors and playgrounds. Perhaps there was a lost coat or jersey, or you missed the bus or you missed having your name called out. The most embarrassing experience for a child is to appear somehow different from the others, to have a raincoat, when everyone else has anoraks, or to have a cap when the other boys are bareheaded. Rather than thinking about how you would like your child to appear or how you might prefer the neighbourhood school to be, your own child's happiness will depend to a large extent upon how well you can both conform to the situation and expectations that really exist. Build on from there.

*Christopher Jarman is a primary school adviser for Oxfordshire county council.*

## bookbox

*Just before school,* M. Chazan, A. Laing and S. Jackson, Blackwell, £2·25.
*Starting school: a study in policies,* R. Palmer, University of London Press, £1.85.
*Time for school: a practical guide for parents of young children,* Cynthia Mitchell, Penguin, 75p.

WHERE on starting school:
Birthday handicap 26, 59
Exhaustion 25
Introduction form for primary schools 47
Need for a new approach (a preview of *Starting School*) 59
Now I am five can I start school? 40
Readiness 10
Teacher's viewpoint 15
What the teacher needs to know 95

# WHAT ABOUT YOU WHEN YOUR CHILD STARTS SCHOOL?

Cynthia Mitchell

Sheelah Latham

'I'VE NEVER TOLD anyone before', said a mother, 'but, that first morning, I went home and wept like a baby. I would never have believed that I could be so silly.' But why should a woman feel foolish if she reacts naturally to unexpected and overwhelming emotion when her child starts school? For caring deeply about what happens to our children is essentially emotional. And the responsibility for infant rearing and infant education still falls largely on women. Their greater involvement makes them aware, sooner than most men, of the emotional strains of parenthood, particularly when a child begins to go to school.

During the years of schooling, the normal, healthy child should develop from a dependent infant to an independent adult. For his parents, the simple matter of adjusting to the alteration in the routine of the family day is the beginning of the very complex matter of both parents adjusting to the lessening of their children's hitherto exclusive dependence upon them. Mothers are usually faced with problems of adjustment sooner than fathers. Experiences like bursting into tears are valuable early warning signs of the danger that, in this process of adjustment, strong feelings about our children can override rational judgement.

Other danger signs for a mother are feeling disappointment if her child doesn't appear to miss her, and feeling pleasure if he does. Children sense when mum expects a few parting tears and often oblige, drying up the moment her back is turned, like the boy in my class who used to say, 'Has she gone round the corner yet?'

**Refilling the empties**

Full-time housewives who have thought, if not screamed out loud, 'Won't I be glad when he gets to school!' are the ones most likely to be prone to lingering in the classroom for their own sakes. When I say, 'I expect you miss him', they invariably answer with apparent relief at being understood, 'Oh I do, I just can't get used to it.' If it is the first child in a family, they often add that the little ones are lost without the elder one. (These bereft little ones are frequently carried out of my classroom kicking and screaming.)

When the only child, or youngest, starts school, mothers speak of the house seeming dead and empty, even uncanny. This is the feeling I remember so well myself, coming downstairs that first day and finding the tidied living room exactly as I had left it. In the static silence of that unbelievable moment, I was shocked to feel panicky rather than delighted by the prospect of more time for myself.

I found that long years devoted to infant rearing can severely sap self-confidence and this can be a long term problem for some mothers.

By contrast, other, no less caring mothers, are truly relieved when children start school. They describe their feelings as 'pure joy' and some just enjoy taking things more leisurely for a change. Others instantly start making up for lost time, tackling jobs neglected in the home, pursuing hobbies, perhaps as remote from the domestic scene as possible (one mother I know successfully took up skin-diving); earning pin-money; resuming interrupted careers or training for new ones (four mothers of children in my present class are beginning teacher training or Open university courses this year).

Some however, find their new enthusiasms more exacting and time consuming than they expected and others begin to worry because they don't miss their children more. When this happens pleasure is marred by guilt. It may be justifiable guilt, but it may be that again the years of child rearing have taken their toll and habits of self-sacrifice become so ingrained that healthy enjoyment feels like self-indulgence. Many caring working mothers of pre-school children suffer such guilt feelings. They may want to spend more time with their children, but have taken perhaps uncongenial jobs because they need the money for what they consider greater priorities. More often than is generally supposed by richer parents, these priorities include feeding and clothing their children and giving them treats as well as other parents seem to do. 'Am I doing right?' working mothers, of all social classes, ask. For the answer, look at the children. If they are thriving the worry is groundless. If they are not, the parents demand more self-sacrifice. But more often than not, the major part will be expected of the mother who may well then find resentment her problem.

Sympathetic understanding leading to practical help from her family and friends can be of inestimable help to a disorientated woman suffering these kinds of emotional strain. But the only advice she so often seems to get is the 'pull-yourself-together' type. 'My husband doesn't understand' is a very common complaint. The attitudes of



From WHERE 108 (September 1975)

husbands are of paramount importance. 'I really will start re-decorating the sitting room this weekend' is more likely to be a short-term face-cheerer than, 'Perhaps you'll get some buttons sewn on my shirts now.'

A woman's need for self-respect as a person in her own right, and not as somebody's mother, wife or dogsbody, is a very real one, and her family will be a happier one if this is recognised before the carrying-over-the-threshold bit, by *both* parents in parenthood. Surely no young woman wants, or ever did want, to develop into the well-known smother-mother, so submerged in her maternal rôle that her very existence seems threatened by any dilution of her family's dependence upon her?

### Disappointments

Then there is the anxiety many parents feel about having to leave their children, often without choice in the matter, in a large group of others in the care of one comparative stranger. Will he settle? Who will protect him from more aggressive children? How will he cope with the demands made upon him? Again, the greatest emotional strain falls on the mother who usually performs the actual act of leaving the children, deals with their excitement, anxiety or distress and first faces a teacher who may not inspire confidence. If, as time goes by, a child is unhappy, or doesn't seem to be learning much, father's emotions become more involved. Something has to be done about it. Parental disappointment arouses anger against the school, followed perhaps by bitterness and bewilderment as the parents find that they are challenging a powerful, imperfect system and rightly or wrongly it is being suggested that they themselves are largely to blame.

Disappointment is something most parents have to face at sometime or other in their children's journey through school. The children, their teacher or the school as a whole may just not live up to a parent's expectations. A parent should look at those expectations, possibly early on in parenthood, and ask how realistic they are. It is not, for example, realistic to assume that a five year old who copies beautifully is necessarily more intelligent than his friend who has difficulty controlling a pencil; nor to expect a teacher with a class of 30 or 40 to have taught a child to read by the end of the first term, or think that the school has deteriorated or that the child is backward if his older sister was an early reader.

Children develop in different ways and at different times. A school may be working with limited resources. A teacher may have specific drawbacks. But recognising limitations is as important as having and expressing expectations. Limitations shouldn't kill expectations, rather they should give the parent a better perspective. Also there is a better chance for the parent to react more rationally and so more effectively about any disappointments that do occur.

### Disjointed

Parenthood is now, largely, a jointly planned venture. There is an increasing tendency to talk of 'the parents' as a single entity. But they never have been and never will be wholly so. For mother and father are two developing people with differing personalities, abilities and upbringings which affect their attitudes towards, and their aspirations for, individual children. A moment of bitter disappointment for one parent can be a moment of 'I-told you-so' triumph for the other. Most teachers have experienced interviews where one parent has seemed reluctant, sometimes fearful, to voice an opinion, or where parents have disagreed violently, usually for the purpose of apportioning blame. At different times, one or the other's views may be dominant. A father who still believes that infant education is solely woman's business may take no interest until later stages. If he then finds that the child has not made as much headway as he expected, he may unfairly blame his wife, who, having been left to struggle with the foundation course alone may then leave all the future decisions to him. Lacking understanding of the early years, the father may then make mistakes of judgement through anger, over-anxiety and perhaps guilt.

Conflicting attitudes towards sex roles can cause many mistakes of judgement. I know of a very clever father who made no secret of the fact that he regarded his wife, and most women, as intellectually inferior. In consequence, he persistently belittled the considerable abilities of a daughter, who happened to look like mother. There are still parents of both sexes who, 'do not believe in higher education for girls', but mothers are usually readier than fathers to recognise how unfairly this limits their daughters' opportunities.

Parents who share fairly the responsibility for their child's vitally important pre-school and subsequent education, who observe how their young children learn and who become as well informed as possible about infant education generally and local schools in particular, can be spared unnecessary disappointment, and are better able to argue the case if they have real cause for complaint. Where good relationships between caring parents and caring teachers can be built up, on a basis of mutual respect and toleration for each other's limitations, parental anxiety and disappointment are minimised.

When children start school parents have not so much lost a child as gained a teacher, with whom the responsibility for their children's education is then shared. Not only will their children still need the support of the home that continues to be the major influence on their lives, but successive teachers will need that support too. If it seems that they are caring alone, teachers, at all stages and of both sexes, will react emotionally too. It is in the nature of our common humanity.

*Cynthia Mitchell is a teacher and a mother. She is the author of the Penguin 'Time for school: a practical guide for parents of young children'.*

Catherine Blackie

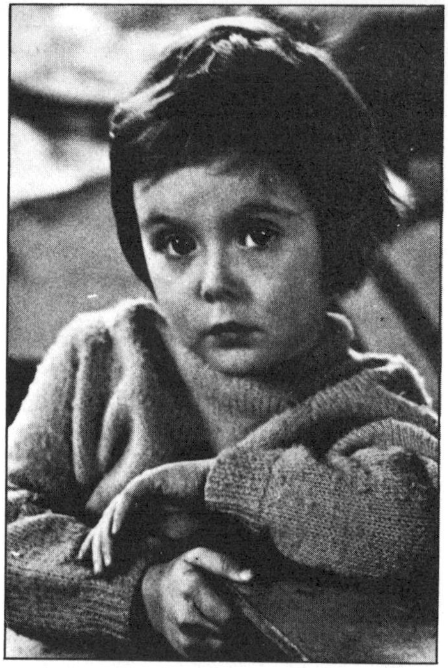

# STARTING SCHOOL: WHAT THE TEACHER NEEDS TO KNOW

## James Hemming

STARTING SCHOOL is a big step forward for a child – and for the mother. It brings a good deal of natural apprehension on both sides. Even when the child has had nursery school or play group experience before five, going to a 'real school' for several hours a day is a new stage. Once the child has reached five he begins to embark upon a road that will take him gradually out into an expanding world of experiences, interests and relationships, culminating in the personal independence of late adolescence. Even mothers who are looking forward to extra hours of freedom may, nevertheless, get a twinge of loss from the feeling that the child is beginning to move away from them. Fathers feel this too.

This new separation may feel very uncomfortable to parents. But it's not very good for the child either. For a start he needs his teacher and parents to share their knowledge and expertise. Nobody *knows* what is ideal for your child. You don't, nor does the teacher. There are no experts in what is best for any particular five year old because every five year old is different from all the others. An experienced teacher will have some well-founded ideas about five year olds in general; so will a mother who has had a lot of contact with young children. And every parent has some knowledge of the particular child. The general and the particular need to come together. About any particular child we cannot know with any certainty; we can only set about finding out. Parents and teachers are both cast in the role of serving the growth of this new individual.

The old-style approach was for parents nervously to regard the teachers as endowed with unlimited expertise, and for the teachers to dismiss the parents as amateurs. These approaches although, unfortunately, still with us, are now outmoded. The most fruitful growth climate for the child is one in which school and home cooperate to bring out the best in him.

Co-operation, as any business man will tell you, is not possible without shared information. Obviously, at the moment when a child enters school, the parents know quite a lot about that child and the teachers, as yet, nothing.

With the passage of time, the teacher will get to know more. But this involves a wait. All along the line, every child needs to feel himself to be understood and appreciated. The logic of this situation is that parents should pass on to the teacher background information that will help the teacher to understand the child right from the start. Teachers do not have X-ray eyes. Just by looking at a child they cannot pick up his story. They need the relevant information about the child that parents can give.

But *what* information? Parents don't want to be fussy, and teachers find perpetually fussy parents troublesome. Firm information however, is *not* fuss. Let me give two examples. Kevin was a lively, able boy who had taught himself to read at the age of four and had acquired some grasp of number because he was interested and his father had enjoyed stimulating the interest. Kevin was put into the reception class where, nothing having been said about his attainments, it was assumed he had to start at the beginning. Kevin was quickly bored and began to play up at school, and about going to school. School, for him, instead of being an exciting opening of doors, was under-stimulating and disappointing.

**Picking up the signals**

The second case concerns John. Little boys are usually frequent visitors to the loo, but John more so than most. He was also shy among strangers about saying when he needed to go. His mother hoped for the best when he went to school but, on the very first day, he wetted himself in the classroom. The teacher soon sorted that one out but the damage had been done. John felt he had lost face and turned against school.

Neither of these difficulties was disastrous. Both were soon put right. But quite unnecessary waste was involved: waste of time, waste of trust, waste of happiness, waste of confidence, waste of relationships. Nor can we ever be sure how far-reaching are the consequences of a bad start. Our aim should be a happy beginning at school for every child. This cannot be achieved if parents are nervous about handing on essential information about their children.

The best way to sort out what is really important from the smaller matters that can be safely ignored is to run through a checklist. The first item on it, as we've already suggested, concerns any attainments which are unusual in a five year old, like being able to read. Any marked interests are also worth mentioning. A child fond of painting

From WHERE 95 (August 1974)

will warm to a school that seems to know what he likes doing. It forms a bond.

Next on our checklist come any unexpected physical features which may lead to difficulties if the teacher is unaware of them. Sight? Hearing? Asthma? A tendency to colds? Infectious diseases safely weathered? Most children, by the time they are five, have a fairly complex medical record of transient ailments. These can be gratefully forgotten. But any physical difficulty that has a bearing on life at school should be passed on to the adults who will now have the care of him.

Emotional and temperamental characteristics also need attention. Infant teachers are trained to expect differences, and will regard as normal a whole range of childish traits that anxious parents may think unusual. All the same, if the child is particularly aggressive or destructive or nervous or retiring or liable to violent tantrums, it is helpful for the school to be forewarned. In passing on information of this kind, parents should aim to be objective about it rather than apologetic. Teachers will understand.

Social development should also come in for consideration. A child of five will only be making a start at mixing and sharing. As a rule, he will enjoy playing in a pair or trio but will begin to get overwhelmed if more is expected of him. Going to school makes a big challenge to his social ability. He will soon respond. Teachers expect to have a lot of steering and encouraging to do and it is useful if they know which children have had previous experience of play groups or nursery schools. These will sometimes be the socially advanced children, who can be helpful as models and guides to the other children. It is also useful for teachers to know about the exceptionally shy ones. They can then direct special attention to bringing these children out.

Next we come to the intimate, important facts of family relationships. In this area the limit is what the parents are prepared to

tell the head teacher, because almost everything is relevant. Whether a child is an only child, adopted, oldest of three, younger of two, or whatever it may be, this will have significance, and will help the school to meet the needs of the child.

The relationships of the parents are also important. Whatever the family situation may be – happy and united, divided and tense, one parent a step-parent, only one parent in the home, or something else – the facts are likely to be known to the school sooner or later and, in the interests of the child, sooner is better than later. The secretive, defensive attitude is out of date. Life is full of hazards. The pretence that we ought all to be perfect in a perfect situation is giving way to the acceptance that actuality falls short of the ideal and that it is better to share our difficulties than to be ashamed of them.

In the modern world, friendly head teachers are finding themselves frequently playing the part of confidants, and it is right that this should be so, because a school can only do its best for a child if relational problems surrounding the child are taken into account.

To share a problem with the head teacher does not mean that intimate facts will be spread around. Without handing on confidential information a head teacher can tell the child's class teacher that she has reason to believe the child is under some strain and that he, or she, needs extra friendliness, encouragement and support. Strain does not imply parental crisis. The arrival of a new baby, or the challenge of a vigorous brother or sister, can be sources of stress for a five year old. Stress at home is likely to work itself out at school, and *vice versa*. To know what are the sources of stress is a great help to reducing, or removing, it.

In this regard, any recent shocks are important: serious illness or hospitalisation for either parent, but particularly for the mother, the death of a well-known relative, divorce, re-marriage and so forth. Such crises are not easy for a five year old to adjust to and the school should know about them. Aggressivity, timid withdrawal, restlessness and slowness in learning can all go back to an unresolved shock in the even tenor of the child's life.

**Checklist**

About five to five and a half is, for many children, a period of consolidating growth when a sense of security and equanimity are especially needed. If, for some reason, they are absent, then the child should be given extra warmth and assurance as compensation. The school can help to supply these – if it knows the facts.

There, then is our checklist:

☐ **attainments and interests**
☐ **physical record**
☐ **emotional and temperamental characteristics**
☐ **social experience and ability**
☐ **family relations**

The objective of running through the check

Richard Dykes

list is, of course, not to manufacture information to pass on to the school, but to make sure that no important items are overlooked.

So much for *what* to communicate. We must now consider *how* it should be communicated. Many schools are careful to enable all new parents to meet the head teacher, or some other responsible person, in circumstances which combine friendliness and confidentiality. But the parent has an important part to play in assuring that this meeting is as fruitful as possible. Many parents find it a help to write down beforehand what they wish to concentrate on. The value of this is twofold: important items are less likely to get left out during discussion, and the teacher has a written record as a reminder.

A good passport-type photograph, with the name of the child written on the back, should always accompany any written statement, or, indeed, any important verbal information also. The value of this is partly to assist memory. Even with a staggered intake, it is not always easy for the head teacher to fit together all the new names and faces at the beginning of the school year. But also, if there is any information about special care to be handed on by the head teacher to a class teacher, it is much easier for the class teacher to help a newcomer effectively and unobtrusively if she has a named photograph with her.

If a school does not provide get-togethers, then the parent is left with the choice of either writing to the head teacher or of arranging an interview – or both. Confidential information, obviously, is best conveyed by word of mouth. Face-to-face contact also permits clarification through question and answer. An interview should always be sought if anything more than an item or two of straightforward information is at issue.

And finally, a warning. We should never talk about a child in the presence of the child except to praise him. I mention this because hard-pressed mums sometimes find it difficult not to take the child along with them when they tell the teacher all about him. This is acutely embarrassing to the child and damages parent-child trust. We should respect the feelings of a child as much as those of a close personal friend.

*James Hemming is a psychologist and writer.*

Roger Mayne

David Rule

# STARTING SCHOOL: A MOTHER-HELPER SCHEME

Viola Wilton

**When a Cornish teacher saw how important it was to involve parents in the school, she did something about it. Which raises the question, why not every school?**

AS A RECEPTION-CLASS teacher a few years ago, I received regular visits from a mother who was anxious about her child Jane's behaviour both at home and in school. Throughout the term, I spent many hours discussing her anxieties, explaining, reassuring, advising – but all to no effect. Finally, in desperation, I suggested that she spend an hour in class to see for herself. The effect was immediate and dramatic:

Oh, I didn't know it was like that. I don't know how you cope with them all. They all seem to like it.

This mother had had the opportunity of seeing her child in relation to her fellows. She saw that Jane was more responsive than most in some ways, less responsive in others, that all the children were free to be themselves and not pressured to conform, and that misbehaviour was regarded as – well, normal! Consequently the mother became more relaxed, confident and encouraging in her attitude. The child blossomed.

I drew two lessons from this incident. Firstly, our discussions had failed to allay the mother's anxiety, whereas her personal experience of the class in action made her understand more immediately what was going on, and what the school was trying to do. Secondly, the mother's tension had adversely affected her child in school. The child was very tense and nervous herself, and would become almost hysterical if the mother was not immediately visible when school was over.

I had understood *some* of the emotional pressures on the child, but had no way of knowing to what extent these disguised her potential and limited her learning. In any case, I was powerless to help her except through helping the mother.

I admire, and am immensely grateful to this mother in her concern for her child; *she* did not 'give up' and her tenacity provoked the solution.

I then began to think of other mothers who might be just as anxious, but were either unable to voice their anxieties, or were afraid that to do so would be regarded as a complaint and possibly antagonise the teacher and make things worse for the child. What could be done about it?

From WHERE 115 (April 1976)

**Learning to adjust**

Infant-school children can have problems in adjusting to school in three areas of difficulty:
*Severe difficulties:* with school phobia, nightmares, psychosomatic illness;
*Intermediate difficulties:* with other children, teachers and headteachers, and with learning;
*Mild difficulties:* with school dinners, PE, toilet facilities.
What is disturbing is that these difficulties tend to decrease very little by the time the children reach 11 years of age. This information of young children's school difficulties has come mainly from parents, and it has been found that many teachers are unaware of these problems.

An increasing number of teachers are now more aware of the needs of children. But many are still unable to communicate children's learning problems to parents, who can so often help to overcome them, or, in some cases, may even inadvertently aggravate the problem. This is certainly not a personal failing by the parents, but rather the result of the confusion created by differing expectations and approaches of parent and teacher, which are made worse when barriers exist between home and school.

For example, a young remedial teacher attempted to reassure a child by encouraging him to talk about his home and to draw his mummy and daddy. The child drew his mother and carefully crayoned her in, but had to be prompted to draw his father, which he left uncoloured. When asked about this, the child said: 'No, I should have to colour it red all over because he's always angry, so I'll leave it.' There was great parental pressure from the parents for this child to do as well as his older brothers. The mother compensated for the father's impatience as much as she could, but this did not solve the problem of the child's ambivalence about his father's behaviour.

In such a situation, it is essential for parent and teacher to discuss together a child's difficulties in learning or in adjusting to school. Even when a child's problem may not be severe, poor communication between home and school can impede progress. But just talking together is often not enough. So the only possibility is to directly involve the mothers (and fathers too, when possible) with their children's school experience.

**Setting up the scheme**

Out of these experiences I decided to set up, with my head's approval, a mother-helper scheme in my reception class. Within two years it had spread throughout the school. All the mothers were invited to share in the teacher's work as a helper, and thus to share in their children's educational experience.

Every term, we introduced parents to the scheme at a party for new children. But to meet the need for information on how the school was organised, we held parents' evenings when each teacher described her approach to the various stages of development reached by the children. Similar meetings had previously been arranged for the PTA, but these had made little impact as parents were not then participating in school life, and had no personal experience to illuminate the verbal explanations.

**What mother-helpers do**

As helpers, the mothers supervise various group activities, painting, modelling, cooking, knitting, sewing and the tuck shop. They help with minor accidents, a sick child, first aid, toilet mishaps; with classroom preparation, cutting paper, mixing glue, sharpening pencils. They offer admiration, stimulate conversation and listen to lengthy stories from children, for which the teacher seldom has enough time. The mothers do not hear readers until basic reading skills have been mastered, then they provide invaluable service in listening and discussing content. This does not apply to each mother's own child, for from the beginning they are free to hear, encourage, admire and discuss all their child's work, including reading.

Regular helpers attend for a morning or afternoon session once a week or fortnight. Some mothers can spare a full day and they stay for school dinners. Morning and afternoon rotas occasionally alternate so that each mother experiences all aspects of the school day. Working mothers are encouraged to take a couple of hours off work at least once a term, and father, grandparents and elder brothers and sisters are welcome as well.

**Problems**

At first, the scheme was very much a matter of trial and error. Mistakes and misunderstandings did occur, but because parents and teachers were working together in the same place, most problems were quickly sorted out, or at least, ameliorated.

A major problem from the mothers' point of view was their feeling of inadequacy and lack of preparation for their role as helpers. The teachers on the other hand, were anxious about the possibility of 'bossy mothers trying to take over the class'. There was a period of mutual adjustment, and as one teacher succinctly said:

> I was unaware . . . of the mothers' feelings and the supreme effort it is for some mothers to come at all. It was only when I appreciated this that I could help them to relax and be themselves which is essential for a fully co-operative relationship. The result is that mothers trust the teacher as a fellow human being and not as a 'superior authority'.

We, the teachers did not fully understand the mothers' anxieties until we asked them to compare their own schooldays with their children's present school experience. We discovered that over three-quarters of them had been unhappy at school, and that over half had been bored and frustrated.

> My memory of infant school was a place where you were taken every day, parents stopped at the gate, were not given much encouragement to participate. I hated it, I remember that. *(Mrs North)*

> So different from my school days that were not the 'happiest days of my life'. *(Mrs Wedlake)*

> I found it very dull being given rows of letters to copy and numbers to add up. These days you seem to do it in such a way that the children learn it very quickly and can see how to put it to a practical use, therefore they are eager to know what is coming next. We did it because we had to even though we could not see where it was leading. *(Mrs Hunkin)*

So one of the most rewarding aspects of the scheme was that the parents discovered that they had a vital contribution to make, that their participation was greatly valued by the staff, and that school could be a happy place.

One major error, from the teachers' point of view, was the initial practice of the mother-helpers and teachers sharing coffee break together. It was found that teachers wanted to consult with colleagues, especially at the relevant times, *eg* 'Did you ever have trouble with "so and so" taking other children's tuck money?' If this was a new occurrence, it may simply be a developmental phase; if it had happened before, the teacher needed to know what action was taken and whether the parents were consulted. The teachers felt that such conversations should be confidential and reflected on their professional responsibility; an unguarded comment in an emergency could cause misunderstanding and distress. So it was agreed that the mothers should remain on duty during playtime, and that they should have their coffee with the head after playtime. This turned out to have advantages, as worried parents took the opportunity of discussing personal problems with the head and of expressing their reactions to their helper role. They were, without exception, enthusiastic and appreciative; they felt 'wanted' and 'part of the school'.

**How it helps**

How does the mother's participation affect a child's educational development? First, as most of the mothers commented, an awareness of modern teaching methods enables them to provide more of the right kind of support:

Being able to see how my child is being educated and the present methods used, this enables me to help him at home in a way which is not contradictory to the way he is being taught at school, so not confusing him with two different methods. *(Mrs North)*

Secondly, the mothers' presence provided increased security and confidence in the children. One mother, Mrs Cloke, explained how it had helped her child 'to settle a lot easier and to join more confidently into school life'. Mrs Bastone was able to provide a useful comparison:

My youngest who had the scheme from reception through to the junior school settled more quickly. She was generally more confident than the eldest who never had the scheme (different school). The middle child had both schools and was far happier with the mother-helper scheme.

Because a mother knew about life at school, her child felt more able to talk about it at home.

I knew what he was talking about with regard to school work, making it less frustrating for him. *(Mrs Timbrell)*

He seems happy that I am familiar with his life at school and I think it is because of this that he talks to me of his day at school. *(Mrs Danders)*

My eldest son did not attend school in this area. I did not know his teacher, his friends or the system of teaching in that school. It was a different world altogether. He told me nothing. Therefore I could not help him. *(Mrs Wright)*

If a child can tell parents about his school, knowing there is a visible, concerned and comprehending link, the learning process can be much more vital and meaningful to that child.

Furthermore, when he is showing work to his parents, he takes the leading role, he is the initiator, he is giving information – himself creating and developing the vital link between home and school, which can provide so much more intellectual stimulation, emotional support and reassurance.

**Other effects of the scheme**

The overall effect of the scheme on the school has been a joint upsurge of creativity and achievement. Parents and teachers combined to build an adventure playground, to organise school visits, bazaars, jumble sales and so on; fathers improve and build equipment, including a sound-proof reading cubicle; parents, teachers and children are all involved in the school assemblies.

One common criticism of parental involvement in schools is that parents are really only interested in their own child's progress. But when this does occur, it is often the result of ignorance engendered by parents' isolation from school life and the anxiety caused by a competitive educational system. As our mothers have clearly and spontaneously demonstrated, when they are truly involved in school life, their interest and concern extends to all the children, and teachers too.

Those parents, who have the opportunity to become part of school life, can help even more by encouraging all mothers to support their children in this way. A doubtful mother may have more confidence if she makes her first visit with a mother who has been there before and knows the ropes. As one of our mothers enthusiastically said: 'The scheme should spread all over Britain'. Several mothers suggested that it should continue into the junior school.

A mother-helper scheme is able to provide a means of community interaction, encouragement and support. It cannot in itself resolve all problems, indeed it often seems that more problems are uncovered. But recognising what are the needs of our children is half the battle. In essence, as parents and teachers, we have only to put the children's needs first. We cannot do so if we are unaware of them.

*Viola Wilton now lectures at the Coventry college of education.*

Dona Haycraft

# Subscribe

**WHERE provides regular information and advice on all aspects of education. It's the monthly education magazine for parents published by ACE at £5·50 a year (£5·25 by banker's order). Write for full details to Dept PSW, Advisory Centre for Education, 32 Trumpington Street, Cambridge CB2 1QY**

**where**